Cross-Cultural Management in Practice

Cross-Cultural Management in Practice

Culture and Negotiated Meanings

Edited by

Henriett Primecz

Corvinus University of Budapest, Hungary

Laurence Romani

Stockholm School of Economics, Sweden

Sonja Sackmann

University of Bw Munich, Germany

Edward Elgar
Cheltenham, UK • Northampton, MA, USA

Published by
Edward Elgar Publishing Limited
The Lypiatts
15 Lansdown Road
Cheltenham
Glos GL50 2JA
UK

Edward Elgar Publishing, Inc.
William Pratt House
9 Dewey Court
Northampton
Massachusetts 01060
USA

Paperback edition 2012

A catalogue record for this book
is available from the British Library

Library of Congress Control Number: 2011929461

ISBN   978 1 84980 407 3 (cased)
         978 0 85793 883 1 (paperback)

Typeset by Cambrian Typesetters, Camberley, Surrey

Printed on FSC approved paper
Printed and bound in Great Britain by Marston Book Services Ltd, Oxfordshire

Contents

Contributors

Guilherme Azevedo recently completed his PhD in Strategy and Organization at McGill University, Montreal, Canada. His research gravitates around the concepts of globalization and culture and includes studies on international business, organizational anthropology, anthropological perspectives of globalization, interpretation of cultures and business development in emerging economies. He has taught at undergraduate and MBA programmes in Brazil and in Canada.

Christoph I. Barmeyer is Professor of Intercultural Communication at the University of Passau, Germany, and Affiliated Professor of Ecole de Management (EM) Strasbourg/University of Strasbourg, France, at the research centre Humans and Management in Society (EA1347). He gained a PhD from the University of Saarbrücken, Germany. He is author of several books and numerous articles in the field of intercultural management, international transfer and international human resource management, with a French-German focus. He also works as a consultant and was board member of Society for Intercultural Education, Training and Research (SIETAR) in Germany, a worldwide association of interculturalists.

Sylvie Chevrier is Full Professor of Management at Université d'Evry Val d'Essonne, France, and a member of the Institut de Recherche en Gestion, the research centre in management of the Université Paris-Est. She obtained a PhD from the University of Quebec at Montreal, Canada, and her main research interests focus on cross-cultural management. She conducts mainly ethnographic research in cross-cultural work situations (European projects, cooperation projects in developing countries, multinational companies). She has published several books on the management of cross-cultural work teams. She is director of a Masters degree course in International Purchases and Distribution.

Lisbeth Clausen is Associate Professor at Copenhagen Business School, Denmark, at the Department of Intercultural Management and Communication and the Vice-Director of the Asian Studies Programme. She is part of the Cultural Intelligence as a Strategic Resource Project in collaboration with Danish multinationals. Her research focus is Japan, where she has lived and carried out research for a decade. Her disciplines of study include media and intercultural communication, Japanese management, business strategy and corporate communication. Her book publications include *Global News Production* (2003, Copenhagen Business School Press) and *Intercultural Corporate Communication: Five Corporate Cases in Japan* (2007, Copenhagen Business School Press), and she has published numerous articles in international journals and encyclopaedia, including *Journal of Scandinavian Management*, *International Journal of Cross Cultural Management*, *Media Culture and Society*, *Nordicom Review*, *Copenhagen Journal of Asian Studies* and *Asian Business and Management Journal*.

Eric Davoine is Professor of Human Resource Management and Intercultural Management at the University of Fribourg, Switzerland. He gained a PhD from the Universities of Freiburg, Germany, and Lyon, France. He has published several books and numerous articles in the field of international human resource management and cross-cultural management, with a French-German focus. He is Vice-President of the Association Francophone de Gestion des Ressources Humanities (AGRH), the association of French-speaking human resource management researchers.

Graham Hollinshead is Reader in International Human Resource Management at the University of Hertfordshire Business School, UK. His main research areas are international and comparative human resource management, international knowledge transfer and cross-cultural management and critical international management studies. His academic work has appeared in *Human Relations*, *Journal of World Business*, *Management Learning* and the *European Journal of Education*. He has acted as consultant to the Deutsche Gesellschaft für Technische Zusammenarbeit (GTZ) and the UN Sponsored European Center for Peace and Development (ECPD) in the upgrading of management capacities in Serbia. He is author of various books and book chapters, including *International and Comparative Human Resource Management* (2009, McGraw-Hill).

Jeanette Lemmergaard is Associate Professor of Strategic Human Resource Management and Internal Communication at the University of Southern Denmark. She is best known professionally for her work on the influence of organizational norms and values on the decision-making processes. She has published in several international journals, including *Employee Relations*, *Journal of Business Ethics* and *Service Industries Journal*. Her current research includes dysfunctional leadership, organizational gossip and psychological work-climate. She is currently working on an edited book with Sara Louise Muhr, *Critical Perspectives on Leadership: Emotion, Toxicity, and Dysfunction* to be published in the New Horizons in Leadership series by Edward Elgar.

Jasmin Mahadevan received her Master's Degree in Languages, Business and Cultural Studies (Diplom-Kulturwirt) with a focus on Southeast Asia from the University of Passau, Germany, and her Doctoral degree in Cultural Anthropology and Intercultural Communication from the Ludwig-Maximilians-University in Munich, Germany. She is Professor of International and Cross-Cultural Management at the School of Engineering, Department of Business Administration and Engineering (BAE), at Pforzheim University, Germany, and Head of the BAE Programme International Management. She also works as an intercultural trainer and consultant for technical companies.

Snejina Michailova is Bulgarian by nationality and holds a PhD degree from Copenhagen Business School, Denmark. She is currently Professor of International Business at the Department of Management and International Business, the University of Auckland Business School, New Zealand. Her main research areas are international management and knowledge management. Her academic work has appeared in *Academy of Management Executive*, *Business Strategy Review*, *California Management Review*, *Employee Relations*, *European Management Journal*, *Journal of Knowledge Management*, *Journal of Management Studies*, *Journal of World Business*, *International Management*, *Management International Review*, *Long Range Planning*, *Management Learning*, *Organizational Dynamics* and other journals. She has edited academic books on knowledge governance (Oxford University Press), human resource management in Central and Eastern Europe (Routledge) and research methodologies in non-Western contexts (Palgrave Macmillan). She was Europe Editor of the *Journal of World Business* from 2001 to 2007 and is currently *Associate Editor of Critical Perspectives on International Business*.

Sara Louise Muhr is a postdoctoral Researcher and Lecturer at Lund University, Sweden, where her research focuses on critical perspectives on managerial identity and business ethics especially in relation to issues around the difficulties of coping with differences and expectations in modern flexible ways of working. Following this broader aim she has worked with various empirical settings such as management consultancy, network organizations and IT companies where she has encountered topics such as work-life subjectivity, gender issues and leadership. She has published in, among others, *Gender Work and Organization*, *Journal of Organizational Change Management*, *Management Decision* and *Journal of Business Ethics*, and has recently published an edited book *Ethics and Organizational Practice – Questioning the Moral Foundations of Management* with Edward Elgar.

Henriett Primecz is Associate Professor at Corvinus University of Budapest, Hungary. Her main research and teaching area are cross-cultural management and organizational theory. Henriett studied business at Janus Pannonius University, Pécs, Hungary, at the Aarhus School of Business, Denmark, and at WU Vienna, Austria. She studied sociology at the Central European University in Warsaw, Poland, and spent two terms at the Judge Institute of Management Studies in Cambridge, UK, during her doctoral research. Henriett gained her PhD from the University of Pécs. She has been teaching Cross-Cultural Management since 1995 in different schools and countries at different levels (BSc, Master, Postgraduate, MBA, PhD) in different programmes. Henriett has published several papers in Hungarian and international journals, for example, *International Journal of Cross-Cultural Management*, *Journal of Asia Business Studies* and *Organizational Research Methods*. She is currently involved in organizing a stream with Loong Wong and Bettina Gehrke for the 7th Critical Management Studies Conference with the theme of 'Critical View Across Cultures'.

Iris Rittenhofer is Associate Professor and head of the Cultural Research Unit at the Department of Business Communication, Business and Social Sciences, Aarhus University, Denmark. She has been educated at six different universities in four countries and publishes in three languages. She has published in several international journals, among them, *Forum: Qualitative Social Research*, *COMPARATIV*, *HERMES* and *NORA*. Her interdisciplinary research interests bring together cultural theories, globalization, market communication and intercultural communication.

Laurence Romani is Researcher at the Centre for Advanced Studies in Leadership, Stockholm School of Economics, Sweden, where she also defended her PhD. Her main research area is cross-cultural management that she studies with a critical perspective. For over ten years, she has taught Cross-Cultural Management with interpretive and critical perspectives, in different universities across Europe. She is currently engaged in a research project on cross-cultural management research and training. In particular, she investigates the theoretical contributions that feminist organizational studies can make to cross-cultural management research, using a bi-paradigm approach. She is also working on the development of pedagogical tools for cross-cultural management education. She recently published *Relating to the Other* (2010, LAP Publishing) and her other publications appear, for example, in *International Journal of Cross-Cultural Management*, *Organizational Research Methods* and several book chapters.

Sonja A. Sackmann has a Chair in Organizational Behaviour at the University Bw Munich, Germany, Department of Economics, Management and Organization Sciences, and is Director of the Institute Developing Viable Organizations. Her research, teaching and consulting focus on corporate/ organizational culture, leadership, intercultural management, personal, team and organizational development in national and multinational contexts. She has published several books, numerous articles in reviewed journals and contributed to handbooks and edited volumes. She taught in the Graduate School of Management at the University of California, Los Angeles, US; St Gallen, Switzerland; Constance, Germany; Vienna, the European Business School (EBS), Austria; and Shanghai, China. She has held positions as Head of Research and Development, Partner and Managing Partner at St Gallen Managementzentrum (MZSG). She received a PhD in Management from the Graduate School of Management at UCLA and an MS and BS in Psychology from the University of Heidelberg, Germany. She was awarded Fulbright and Deutscher Akademischer Austausch Dienst (DAAD) Scholarships, the Wechsler Fund Award, the Glady's Byram Fellowship and the best paper award from the Western Academy of Management.

Sampo Tukiainen is Project Manager and Researcher at the Aalto University School of Economics, Finland, where he also received his PhD in 2011. His PhD thesis focused on the constructions of Finnish cultural identity in cross-cultural interaction, building on the experiences of project managers of large-scale, international engineering projects. He is currently a project manager in a large European Union-funded research project, which is focused on developing cross-cultural innovation networks. His current and future research interests lie in applying the cultural perspective to studying project management and start-up companies, as well as military hierarchies and leadership. His research interests also include management consulting and mergers and acquisitions.

Hèla Yousfi is Associate Professor in the Department of Management and Organization at Paris Dauphine University (DRM), France. She received her PhD from the University of Nanterre at Paris in 2006. She is specialized in the field of sociology of organizations. She teaches graduate courses on cross-cultural management, strategic management and organization theory. She has conducted research and published on the topic of culture and management practices transfer in North Africa and the Middle East, including Lebanon, Jordan, Egypt, Tunisia, Algeria and Morocco. She is also an experienced trainer in intercultural management. Her work has also centred around issues such as culture, institutions and economic development, trust and cross-cultural cooperation and culture in critical management perspectives.

Acknowledgements

We benefited from the contributions and support of a number of people and institutions in developing and writing this book and we would like to take this opportunity to offer our thanks.

First of all, we would like to thank the contributors' excellent input and hard work in this task. They follow us in our endeavour to build a coherent book from the diverse, interesting and strong papers they first wrote. We know how hard or even painful it is to cut a good paper into almost half. Despite this, we asked them to do so because we believe together with the publisher that for teaching purpose short cases are best suited. Several times this meant asking the authors to rewrite a different summary of the empirical material and the analysis, in addition to implications for practitioners. We are thankful for the contributors' willingness to receive and consider our editorial comments, for the energy they put in the rewriting process and finalization of the chapters into a coherent unity. Thank you.

During the process of finalizing the volume, we asked and received feedback from different academic audiences. First of all, the contributors to this volume helped us to finalize the introduction, the first chapter and the closing (12th) chapter with constructive comments and suggestions. A special thanks goes to Guilherme Azevedo's detailed comments. We are grateful to colleagues who read parts of the book and contributed to the development of the volume with their valuable comments. Thank you Anne-Marie Søderberg for your careful reading and suggestions. Thank you András Gelei for your insights on how to write an accessible yet accurate brief presentation of interpretive research. Thank you Betina Szkudlarek for your supportive comments and suggestions on how to better adjust the chapters to the needs of a student audience. Jesper Blomberg, Johan Berglund, Mats Tyrstrup and Ingela Sölvell, thank you for the inspiring comments and discussions you initiated around the draft of Chapter 1. Thank you Sára Csillag for your enlightning comments on structure.

We are also grateful to several institutions that supported us during the writing process. Laurence Romani was visiting researcher at the Department of Organization and Personnel Management, Rotterdam School of Management when the bulk of the editorial work and the draft of three chapters were done. Thank you Sławomir Magala for making this stay possible and warmly supporting the realization of this volume. Thank you Anne-Marie Søderberg for inviting Laurence to the Department of Intercultural Communication and Management, Copenhagen Business School during the finalization of Chapter 1 and the stimulating conversations that contributed to further enrich the chapter. We would also like to thank Silke Agricola of the University Bw Munich for her work regarding the layout of the chapters and identifying inconsistent as well as missing references. This volume is part of a larger research project on cross-cultural management research and education. Our gratitude goes to Vetenskapsrådet, the Swedish Research Council, for its financial support of the project called 'The Hidden Side of Cross-Cultural Management' (project number 421-2009-2020). Laurence Romani would not have been able to contribute to this volume without their support.

Introduction

This book is a collection of ten cases that deal with real life cross-cultural issues and also discusses implications for practitioners. The cases are based on field research revealing challenges and benefits from working across countries. In a succinct way, they provide both illustrations and insights on how to deal with actual cross-cultural issues. Topics cover, for example, international collaboration across organizations and within multinational companies, organizational culture in international joint ventures, as well as knowledge transfer.

WHAT ARE THE USES AND BENEFITS OF THE BOOK?

Practice-oriented studies on intercultural interactions have been repeatedly called for, because students and practitioners often consider predefined constructs or cultural dimensions too abstract, remote from practice, or lacking recommendations for dealing with and solving intercultural conflicts and misunderstandings (Blasco, 2009; Cant, 2004; Earley and Peterson, 2004; and more generally Burke and Rau, 2010). Influential models such as Hofstede's (1980) cultural dimension framework have been developed for cultural issues at the national level of analysis and for the purpose of comparing national cultures. The implications of these models for interactions in practice are not straightforward. When working together, people need to find concrete and creative solutions that help them deal with their differences; they need to go beyond the comparison of management practices across countries. Consequently, this volume provides cases that show how organizational members deal with their differences by mutually constructing their social reality, thus overcoming – or augmenting – their culturally based differences. In addition, the concluding chapter summarizes major insights from the cases and proposes nine strategies on how to successfully handle cultural differences and their related dynamics in practice.

WHAT ARE THE CONTRIBUTIONS OF THIS EDITED VOLUME?

While editing this book we worked with the authors to condense their findings into accessible and readable texts for the benefit of students and practitioners alike, without compromising on theoretical and methodological rigour.

Ten Cases Showing Cross-cultural Management in Practice

The results are ten succinct and straight-to-the-point cases. They bridge theory and practice, they are close to the experienced reality of people and thanks to interpretive investigations they show how theoretical constructs apply in practice. The cases present success and failure stories in cross-cultural management. The qualitative in-depth studies display situated knowledge along with the participants' own explanations and are thus a rich source of inspiration. Although such studies are published in academic journals, an edited volume for students and practitioners, containing rich qualitative case studies, has been missing since Sackmann (1997).

A Contribution to the Theoretical Framework of Culture and Negotiated Meanings

By offering a study of a German-Japanese joint venture, Brannen and Salk (2000) contributed to confirm the idea that (organizational) culture emerges and develops through interactions between members of different cultural groups rather than being the juxtaposition or imposition of one culture onto the other. The emergent culture is called a 'negotiated culture'. In this volume, we consider not only partners who are present and negotiating to find an agreement, but also individuals and groups actively reinterpreting their environment, or aspects of this environment, and thus taking part in the very dynamics of cultural changes.

A Power Perspective for the Study of Cross-cultural Interactions

We argue that the power balance between interacting partners needs to be addressed because this balance (or the lack of it) affects how culture and cultural differences are talked about and how meanings are negotiated through interactions. Moreover, since power is often implicitly present, participants of intercultural interactions and researchers do not necessarily address it; instead they try to explain misunderstandings, conflicts or smooth relations with cultural reasons. Power discrepancies can exist between headquarters and subsidiaries, between different professional groups in an organization, or they can take the form of opposition between technical knowledge and client knowledge. Openness towards others and willingness to take their view into account will partly depend on people's power position in the intercultural relationship.

Nine Strategies for Effective Intercultural Interactions

The learning we can derive from these cases is condensed in the last chapter of this volume into a model presenting nine strategies for effective intercultural interactions. These strategies address expectations, understanding and actions to be considered when dealing with multiple cultures in practice. The model takes into account both the people involved in interaction and their environment. It provides a guide in intercultural situations where negotiation of meaning and power imbalance are part of the interaction.

OVERVIEW OF THE CHAPTERS

In the first chapter we introduce the reader to the philosophical and methodological background of studying culture in an interpretive way and we underscore that this approach differs from the assumptions and knowledge developed by the use of cultural dimension constructs. Using illustrations from the ten case studies, we describe the theoretical framework of this volume. First, we explicate the view that meaning is negotiated and that culture is socially constructed and reinterpreted in interaction. Second, we present the construct of 'meaning system' as an alternative to cultural dimensions, hitherto among the few available tools to talk about cultural differences across countries. Finally, we insist on the need to consider power imbalance in cross-cultural interactions, since it is an influential part in the negotiation of meanings.

The first case by Sara Louise Muhr and Jeanette Lemmergaard (Chapter 2) reports a study of an individual consultant travelling from his North-European home to developing countries. The frequent traveller's challenge is how to deal with constantly changing work environments and varying cultural influences. While constantly on the road, rarely in familiar places, he has to struggle with solitude and constant change in addition to his work. Muhr and Lemmergaard argue convincingly that spaces of generic culture – so-called 'non-places' – provide cross-cultural workers with a sense of familiarity and identity. Airports and airplanes can be similar all over the world, they do not impose a specific culture, requiring little attention to read and understand the place once a person is familiar with the generic setting. It is these non-places that cross-cultural workers can use to cope with working across multiple cultures.

In Chapter 3, Sampo Tukiainen presents collaboration between a Finnish parent company and a Polish subsidiary in two large infrastructural projects. The case offers a report of a successful earlier collaboration and investigates how it is possible that conflicts emerged in a second project involving the same group of people. It reveals that beyond cultural differences, individual and organizational strategic interests collided. The Finnish headquarters brought the technical know-how to the Polish partner who actually had an advantage in local market knowledge, managers had divergent agendas and both organizations wanted to lead the project. This case underscores the problematics related to the possibilities for automatically extending prior success to future collaboration. It is also an example of collaboration between members of a Western country and a post-socialist one after the economic and political transition.

The case in Chapter 4 deals with collaboration between French and Vietnamese partners in the context of a non-governmental organization (NGO). Employees from both countries work together on development projects, such as services to farmers, reducing malnutrition and micro-finance. Sylvie Chevrier describes the possibilities of smooth cooperation, although the partners had very different views, for instance, on individual autonomy, empowerment and work ethics. French workers assumed that close supervision was a sign of lack of trust; this is why they gave autonomy and expected initiative from their Vietnamese colleagues. In contrast, their colleagues found them distant, offering little support and exchange on details of the project. At the same time, the Vietnamese were seen by their French partners as incoherent when they were respectful of the social rules of their communities. The author shows that divergences in sense-making systems are at the root of the misunderstandings and she explains how to reach a position that values and builds on this cultural diversity.

The case by Christoph Barmeyer and Eric Davoine (Chapter 5) explores the transfer of codes of conduct from the American headquarters to French and German subsidiaries. The authors underscore that it is not only cultural differences and legal frameworks that influence the interpretation and thus the adoption of the code; they also show that other issues need to be considered such as the kind of relationship between headquarters and subsidiaries, or the presence and intent of active unions. They reveal that despite the successful diffusion and official adoption of the code, the code has a different ethical and legal value in France and Germany, or none at all, because adaptations to local legal frameworks were not made.

In Chapter 6, Hèla Yousfi addresses the tension between diffusion of universal management systems, or best practices, and the need for local adaptations. The case presents a successful introduction of 'American' management techniques in a Tunisian company. On closer examination the interviews show, however, that the very success of the introduction of these techniques depended on their reinterpretation in terms of a 'Tunisian' sense-making system. The author highlights that the techniques used were able to meet locally defined expectations of 'good management' and to overcome deficiencies in certain local business practices. The case illustrates the potential implications of globalization, as well as the importance of local culture and the adaptation of global methods to a local context.

Another success story is the interaction between a Danish company and its Japanese subsidiary after fundamental changes in the company's market strategy (Chapter 7). Lisbeth Clausen analyses the collaboration through the lens of communication and shows the different levels of communication between the parties involved. She reveals the negotiations taking place between the headquarters and the subsidiary, and the various levels of culture (national, professional and so on) that influence their interaction. This case also points to societal trends in Japan and to the important role played by bicultural persons who can act as translators between people from both cultures.

The case by Jasmin Mahadevan in Chapter 8 shows that cross-cultural work is not only happening at the national level and that the cultural boundaries that one needs to bridge are also changing. The case deals with collaboration between German and Indian engineers who apparently denied and minimalized their national cultural differences, and stressed in contrast their shared professional culture. The author opens our eyes to the cultural dynamics that come into play at different levels: the national (Indian versus German) and the professional level (engineers versus managers and human resources professionals). She also reveals that these boundaries are changing depending on the context. For example, she shows how in a period of uncertainties, German engineers could change their discourse and present Indian engineers as being very different and becoming a threat for the future of engineers in the German sites.

Chapter 9 relates to a project directed to Eastern Europe in the early 1990s, just after the political and economic transitions. Bulgaria was supported by Western European states as the beneficiary of a programme providing management education. Snejina Michaliova and Graham Hollinshead show that the very first part of the project was a sort of blind drive: the educator had neither information of the knowledge that was needed or the knowledge that participants already had, nor did they have any local knowledge. The case addresses fundamental issues linked to knowledge transfer and reveals how the project gradually changed the form of knowledge that was transmitted to become more successful.

In Chapter 10, Guilherme Azevedo reports of two joint ventures between Chinese and Brazilian organizations. He shows that intercultural cooperation is feasible despite large cultural differences (China and Brazil can be seen as cultural antipodes). Based on ethnographic observation, the author suggests that effective cooperation can be built upon the construction of a sense of proximity and through micro-dynamics of integration. Although the informants acknowledge that interactions between people with such different cultural backgrounds may not always be easy, they indicate that good intentions and the dynamics of their concrete actions can eventually lead to fruitful cooperation and a successful joint venture.

Chapter 11 offers an analysis of 'globalization' in corporate language use, denoting ways of thinking and perceiving the transforming relations between home and foreign markets. Iris Rittenhofer explores shared cultural patterns of perceptions and meaning production through two cases: the visualization of a global company and the discourse of an expert advising how to prepare for global markets. Unravelling these perceptions of globalization, she shows implications for strategy development processes: the way organizations see (or imagine) foreign markets will impact their globalization process.

In the closing Chapter 12 we summarize the managerial and practical implications of the ten cases and propose nine strategies for dealing with inter- and cross-cultural differences at work. These include expecting differences rather than similarities when different cultures are involved and we stress that cultural frames that are in a given context need to be identified and understood from the perspective of the native participants. Acting as an interpreter and translator of meaning may foster mutual understanding and such practice may be aided by identifying and building on common grounds. Respect for others is important while refraining from judgment, appreciating existing differences and learning from them add value to cross-cultural work. At the same time a common vision, purpose or goal will help overcome cultural differences while working towards that shared goal. Next to these strategies it is also important to be aware of the larger context in which interactions take place.

HOW DID THIS BOOK COME TO BE?

The three editors are themselves boundary spanners between different academic domains and divergent cultures. Familiar with both the fields of organization studies and international management, we could see similarities and points of contact between these two academic fields. One important link is the study of the interconnection of culture and management. This topic has been well researched both in the positivist paradigm with cultural dimension frameworks, and in the interpretive paradigm with intercultural interaction studies. Yet, few cross-references exist and consequently very limited cross-fertilization between these two streams of research. Our object became to raise the awareness of the importance and value of different paradigms among researchers working with culture and management, by revealing how many different streams and research traditions currently exist (see Primecz et al., 2009). Together with Katalin Topçu, we organized a track at the European Group for Organizational Studies annual conference in Vienna (EGOS 2007) that led later to a call for papers for the special issue of the

International Journal of Cross-Cultural Management (issue 3, volume 9, 2009). In both instances, we received a large number of submissions, most of them submitted by interpretive researchers. This is when our idea of an edited volume started. We wanted to promote the visibility of interpretive research in cross-cultural management and provide hands-on, applied cases and illustrations of cross-cultural management that could be used for teaching purposes. We actively worked on completing the range of studies represented in this volume to include cases related to various geographical locations (North and South America, Europe, Africa and Asia) and treated by researchers of various origin (Europe, South America and Africa) and interpretive research traditions.

Our professional training, teaching, research and consulting experiences have influenced this volume in many ways, starting from the various networks in which we diffused the call for papers, to the goal we had of including cases linked to rarely covered geographical areas (such as Eastern Europe or North Africa). We hope that our edited volume will not only provide exciting reading but also become a useful resource for practitioners, students of cross-cultural management, and colleagues alike.

REFERENCES

Blasco, M. (2009) 'Cultural pragmatists? Student perspectives on learning culture at a business school', *Academy of Management Learning & Education*, **8**(2), 174–87.

Brannen, M.Y. and J. Salk (2000), 'Partnering across borders: negotiating organizational culture in a German-Japanese joint venture', *Human Relations*, **52**(4), 451–87.

Burke, L.A. and B. Rau (2010), 'The research-teaching gap in management', *Academy of Management Learning and Education*, **9**(1), 132–43

Cant, A.G. (2004), 'Internationalizing the business curriculum: developing intercultural competence'. *Journal of American Academy of Business*, **9**, 177–82.

Earley, P.C., and R.S. Peterson (2004), 'The elusive cultural chameleon: cultural intelligence as a new approach to intercultural training for the global manager'. *Academy of Management Learning and Education*, **3**, 100–15.

Hofstede, G. (1980), *Culture's Consequences: International Differences in Work-Related Values*, Beverly Hills, CA: Sage.

Primecz, H., L. Romani and S.A. Sackman (2009), 'Cross-cultural management research: contributions from various paradigms', *International Journal of Cross-Cultural Management*, **9** (3), 1–8.

Sackmann, S.A. (ed.) (1997), *Cultural Complexity in Organizations: Inherent Contrasts and Contradictions*, Newbury Park, CA: Sage.

1. Culture and negotiated meanings: the value of considering meaning systems and power imbalance for cross-cultural management

Laurence Romani,* Sonja A. Sackmann and Henriett Primecz

What can we expect when a Brazilian and a Chinese company decide to form a strategic alliance and, for the first time in their corporate history, develop a joint-venture project? We imagine significant cultural differences, potential clashes due to their dissimilar national and organizational cultures, and the risk of a premature termination of the venture (based on, for example, Hofstede, 2001; Barkema and Vermeulen, 1997). Similarly, when a German organization transfers some of its technical operations to India, we understand that the personnel department in Germany would argue in support of cross-cultural management training for the engineers who would be working most closely with their counterparts in India. In addition, when we learn of the success of a project between the headquarters in Finland and its subsidiary in Poland, we expect their second collaboration also to run smoothly. The case studies included in this edited volume will demonstrate that, in practice, these expectations may be misleading.

BEYOND CULTURAL DIMENSIONS

These expectations may be misleading because they are based upon assumptions and knowledge that do not apply in the respective situations. These expectations rest quite frequently upon the notion of culture that has been developed in the international management literature. For example, they suggest that North Americans are individualistic and Chinese are collectivistic, that culture can be measured, and that it has an impact upon human behaviour in predictable ways. This abundant literature on cross-cultural dimension frameworks (see Nardon and Steers, 2009 for a review) has revealed the influence of culture on management (see Kirkman et al., 2006). The literature also shows the differences in practices and preferences between countries on a national level of analysis, as well as how its instruments enable comparisons between countries. In brief, cultural dimension frameworks (such as Hofstede, 1980, 2001; House et al., 2004, Trompenaars, 1993; Schwartz, 1994) aim to compare national cultural differences on a general level; however, they cannot adequately predict or explicate what happens when people actually meet and interact with each other.

In this volume, you will find the case of successful intercultural integration in two Sino-Brazilian joint ventures. It underlines the fact that, depending upon the situation and one's specific agenda, people may or not wish to emphasize cultural differences. This implies that knowing about cultural differences (such as the ones depicted in the cultural dimension constructs) does not suffice in predicting and managing cultural clashes or the lack thereof. Another case shows that German engineers resisted cross-cultural management training because they identified with Indian engineers. They saw them as fellow engineers and colleagues, and did not see a need for explicitly addressing cultural differences between the two countries. We learn in another case that, despite the similarities in partners and projects, a successful inter-cultural collaboration is no guarantee of future success. This chapter (among others in this volume) also reveals that when people talk about cultural differences they do not necessarily mean the differences as suggested in cultural dimension constructs; they imply and express power inequalities instead.

A FOCUS UPON INTERACTION RATHER THAN COMPARISON

Cultural dimension constructs are used foremost for comparisons. They inform us about an average behaviour or preference in a given country; however, they are limited, if not misleading, when used to explicate interactions. When employees of Chinese and Brazilian companies begin working together, they are not 'comparing' themselves with each other; they are interacting with each other and trying to solve the issues at hand. Although they are, indeed, influenced by their cultural background(s), individuals do not mechanistically enact their country's culture scores upon researched cultural dimensions. So what do they do? We shall demonstrate that they negotiate.

By introducing the notion of culture and negotiated meanings, and using examples taken from previous research and the ten case studies, this chapter provides the theoretical framework for the volume. We first explain that our approach is interpretive, and focuses upon interactions; this means that it builds upon very different assumptions and research methods than the cultural dimension literature. In our approach, cultural differences between countries are explained by the construct of meaning systems. Since we focus upon inter-actions, we argue that power issues need to be considered in order to under-stand cross-cultural management in practice.

THE ADVANTAGE OF USING AN INTERPRETIVE APPROACH

There are many advantages of using an interpretive approach to cross-cultural management: for example, a focus upon interactions and, thus, actual inter-personal management practices (a level of analysis that is closer to our experienced reality rather than a mean for a nation) and investigation methods accessible to individual managers. We shall further address this latter point below.

Consider, for example, an international business negotiation meeting. Using a questionnaire and video recording, we can collect a large amount of data that reveals information about the purpose of the meeting, the place, the profiles of the persons in interaction, as well as specifics about verbal and non-verbal interactions. This is very rich and valuable information; however, if we also consider meanings attached to this meeting, we gain a very different picture. For example: what did a negotiation meeting mean for the different partners? Was the meeting equally important to all the persons in interactions? Were there previous meetings and how did the participants experience those? What is associated with the meeting location: did the meeting take place on neutral ground? How do the participants relate the arguments advanced by the other party, and what were the consequences? This example points to the advantage of adding the investigation of meanings to the study of human inter-actions since they are both tangible and critical parts of their actions. This highlights the influence of the context upon the interaction, the significance of the interaction, the potential power struggles and many other aspects that participate directly or indirectly to what is happening at the meeting.

A questionnaire is a powerful research tool; however, it is made of pre-defined questions and builds upon categories that do not necessarily fit with the respondents' points of view. Value surveys are also compelling means of investigation, yet they cannot tell us how people actually enact these values in, for example, an intercultural interaction. Conversely, participant observation and interviews allow us to come closer to what people do and how they think in practice. Human beings constantly interpret what is going on around them; they use meanings to make sense of what they are experiencing, and their current and future actions are based upon these interpretations. Therefore, it is essential to understand the meanings with which people associate what they do, the situation in which they find themselves, and the way in which their partner acts and reacts to what it is that they are doing. Accessing these meanings requires investigating how people make sense of what is going on around them, and requires an interpretive approach.

INTERPRETIVE CROSS-CULTURAL MANAGEMENT RESEARCH IN A NUTSHELL

Interpretive research is rich in diverse streams and methods (see Alvesson and Sköldberg, 2000; Guba and Lincoln, 2005; Hatch and Yanow, 2003) that cannot be addressed in this brief introduction. We choose to focus upon defining characteristics of interpretive cross-cultural management research, especially those in contrast to cultural dimension constructs.

Unravelling and Understanding the Actors' Perspectives

The centre of the analysis in interpretive studies is people embedded in their socio-cultural reality: their experience, their ways of thinking, their sense-making and how they talk about it – that is, their lifeworld.[1] Researchers endeavour to see the world through the eyes of the people whom they are investigating, grasping the rational of their actions and making sense of them (as in *Verstehen*[2]). They aim to comprehend the insider's view, since this view is indicative of the socio-cultural reality of the person and, thus, of the society in which she lives. One consequence of this is that researchers are not concerned about whether the sense given by the person(s) is either the right or the best one. The aim is not to reach an external and generalizable knowledge; rather, it is to unravel and understand the world from the perspective of the acting persons, situated in their own local context and, therefore, understanding the society in which they live.

As an example, a multinational company had tried repeatedly to implement Total Quality Management (TQM) in its Moroccan subsidiary when it suddenly worked in a very successful way. The investigation by d'Iribarne (2002) reveals that this change was triggered by the employees' new interpretation of the TQM principles. Was it the 'correct' interpretation, in line with the context in which it had been developed in Japan? The answer is not at all; however, the implementation of TQM was no less successful. The employees' new interpretation referred to the 'Zaouia' (a pre-Islamic form of community), which stands for a community with a strong (exemplary) leader and moral principles. This happened when a new chief executive officer (CEO) personally and rigorously applied the TQM principles and when a parallel was drawn during corporate training between TQM principles and precepts of the Qu'ran. This combination of an exemplary leader (new CEO), moral guidance (TQM and Qu'ran principles) with a community (the organization) resulted in employees using the metaphor of the Zaouia and successfully adopting and implementing TQM.

Interpretive researchers do not test a theory or a model with hypotheses that either will or will not be supported. Instead, the definition of the investigated problem, and the relevant constructs and meanings emerge: the interpretive researchers progressively understand and develop them. Researchers who were investigating the adoption of TQM in this Moroccan organization did not know in advance about the implicit use of the metaphor of the Zaouia. By carefully listening and analysing the way employees were talking, researchers progressively came to this explanation.

The outcome of interpretive works can be seen as transferable (Guba and Lincoln, 2005) rather than generalizable. The adoption of TQM principles across the world is not linked to the Zaouia; this result is not generalizable. However, the revealed adoption process is transferable: employees are more likely to adopt TQM when its principles and implementation can be interpreted and understood in a culturally meaningful way. The case by Hèla Yousfi presented in Chapter 6 underlines the same process: 'foreign' management practices are successfully implemented when employees can (re)interpret them in a (culturally) meaningful way (see also the work by Brannen, 2004 on recontextualization).

Meanings are Dynamic and Emerge in Context

The meanings people give to a situation are socially constructed and depend upon the context. Irrmann (2008) gives the example of a failed negotiation between Finnish and French interlocutors, even though all premises for success were present. The French seller confronted by the silence of the Finnish client interpreted it as an act of suspicion and hesitation. The French seller tried harder to convince the Finnish client who, in turn, interpreted this very act in a negative way. In fact, silence in itself does not mean anything: the sense – or meaning – of silence is socially constructed. It means what we have learned to associate it with, and the sense that people in an interaction tend to give to it. Irrmann argues that it is a common communication pattern in Finland to remain silent for some time in order to show consideration for what has been said, thereby, showing interest. He points out that another pattern tends to prevail among French interlocutors: interruption, instead of silence, indicates interest. The interpretation of an action or a situation is partly linked to the socially constructed meanings attached to it and partly to individual meanings: the meanings we give from our personal life experience and identity. Individual meanings develop over time: through socialization in various settings and groups (such as a family, gender, religion, town, nationality, profession and so on). Meanings that develop in an interaction are, thus, embedded in their context (social and personal); they are socially constructed.

The context of the interaction is meaningful, as is the way in which interviewees tell their story. In the study of expatriate tales about cultural encounters, Gertsen and Søderberg (2010) show how narrating – telling the story of a particular event – is not neutral. This is a social act, a retrospective interpretation, which often takes part in identity construction (see also Søderberg, 2006). Sara Louise Muhr and Jeanette Lemmergaard use this approach as an example (see Chapter 2). The stories of an international consultant reveal how he copes with being an outsider and insider simultaneously. He uses 'non-places' (airport lounges, international hotel rooms, in other words, impersonal spaces) to preserve his identity. The narration of his assignments is not a neutral descriptive story; it is also a story structured around – and influenced by – his use of space (culturally embedded and non-places) and his identity issues. In sum, researchers need to consider the context of the interview, the way in which the story is told, who is the storyteller and in which context the story told has taken place. Therefore, there are always multiple 'contexts' to be considered and they are all parts of meanings.

Interpretive studies pay attention to processes because interactions are dynamic. The way in which people make sense of what is happening is dynamic; the context may be changing and former interactions influence the new ones. For example, Snejina Michailova and Graham Hollinshead show us in Chapter 9 that the content of management training delivered in Bulgaria after the fall of the Berlin wall changed subsequently from a perspective of simple knowledge transfer from Western Europe to Eastern Europe to a much stronger involvement of local meanings. Meanings such as good management and entrepreneurship are not transmitted; rather, they are (re)created and negotiated. Meanings are always in a process of becoming since they depend strongly upon the context of the exchange. For example, entrepreneurship in Eastern Europe in the 1990s did not mean the same as it did in Western Europe; it most certainly did not have the same positive connotations. Trainers needed to adapt to the local context, and to the local reality of the trainees. Trainers and trainees developed the forms of knowledge that were transmitted. In sum, interactions are a dynamic process, leading to a change in sense-making and meanings throughout this process.

In Dialogue

Meanings cannot be collected by controlled observation of behaviour (such as in a laboratory), nor can they be collected by large-scale questionnaire studies: they emerge in dialogue. Researchers need to ask people, learn to understand the words they use and the meanings attached to them in the specific contexts of the interaction, observe how the subjects utilize or organize their environment and so on. This implies that interpretive studies apply predominantly qualitative methods (such as interviews, participant observations, text analysis and narrative analyses[3]). Since meanings are not directly accessible, it is through a dialogue with expression that we can reach them, that is to say, words, images, organization of space, time or discourse. In a text, meanings are implicit and the researcher needs to progressively bring underlying meanings systems to the forefront. This can be done in a dialogue, including the contexts and the text. The researcher asks questions and searches for answers, taking into consideration the contexts in which the text has been developed as we have shown in the previous section. Researchers gain a preliminary understanding in this interaction with the text and continue their dialogue until they have reached interpretations (Alvesson and Sköldberg, 2000, p. 62) that are found to be relevant and convincing to interviewees or other researchers.

In Chapter 10, for example, Guilherme Azevedo wants to understand the successful cultural integration of Sino-Brazilian organizations. A preliminary question is: why did cultural integration happen in their case when it did not in so many other collaborations? A causality expressed by the Chinese interviewees is: 'working with Brazilians is easier … because we treat each other as being on the same level'. The interpretive analysis predominantly searches for patterns rather than causality and explanation (Alvesson and Sköldberg, 2000, p. 61). Consequently, the researcher does not stop at the interviewees' explanation of causality, but searches for similar ways in which interviewees organize their respective narratives. Guilherme Azevedo demonstrates that the members of the international joint venture develop shared meanings that Chinese and Brazilians are closer to each other than one might usually expect. This pattern appears repeatedly in the observation notes and transcriptions of the interviews. But how does this sense of proximity contribute to the cultural integration? By continuously interrogating the text and its context of production, Guilherme Azevedo shows that this sense of proximity supports the micro-dynamics of integration, thus, the actual cultural integration of the organization.

Since 'texts' are, for example, the transcriptions of interviews and notes on what one has observed in the field or on what informants have said in informal conversations, this method is very accessible to practitioners in contrast to large databases. In their interactions with colleagues or clients, practitioners can develop the technique of dialoguing with this 'text', by carefully listening to what people are saying, posing questions and observing what people actually do. They need to go beyond the spoken words and search for patterns. For example, Romani (2010) shows that Japanese interviewees repeatedly say that their Swedish superiors are being nice. This is a pattern. Questioning this pattern requires asking what the interviewees actually mean by the word 'nice' during, for example, a lunch conversation. A second pattern then emerges: a 'nice' supervisor is contrasted with a 'directive' one. The next step is then to ask the interviewees (and their 'text') what they mean by 'directive'. Moving from one pattern to the next, a clearer picture progressively emerges informing us about the Japanese interviewees' views on leadership.

Reflexivity

Reflexivity is used by interpretive researchers to investigate how their text (data) has been collected and analysed. They systematically think about the conditions of their research during the investigation, their choice of theory, the way in which they use theory and their analyses. In brief, they critically and consciously reflect upon every aspect that is part of their research, which influences their analyses and the conclusions they reach. In order for their conclusions to be accepted as relevant, researchers need to show this reflexivity to the same extent as statisticians need to detail their analyses. Reflexivity is a key aspect in the development of interpretive analysis; it is a necessary condition for validity and reliability.

In order for managers to better understand meanings while conversing with their employees in a corporate environment, it is also important to perform this reflexivity. Under what conditions did the conversation take place? Could the person talk freely or did the hierarchical difference impede what was said? What was surprising or touching during the interview? Why did I draw this conclusion after the interview? Do other colleagues share my opinion? These are some of the questions that can help you begin a reflective process.

In this succinct presentation of the interpretation of texts and the search for meanings, we have underlined a number of aspects, such as the centrality of the lived experience, the meanings attached to it, the importance of contexts, the necessity to search for patterns in texts and researchers' reflexivity. These are central aspects of interpretive research, such as those presented in the following case studies. The theoretical framework of culture and negotiated meanings is yet another.

CULTURE AND NEGOTIATED MEANINGS

The study of interactions between different cultures in management studies encouraged a view on culture as being dynamic. For example, with the negotiated culture approach.

The Negotiated Culture Approach

Inspired by the concept of negotiated order (see Strauss, 1978), the negotiated culture approach posits 'patterns of meanings and agency in the organization arise from the interactions and negotiations of its members' (Brannen and Salk, 2000, p. 456). Brannen and Salk (2000) show that members of a German–Japanese joint venture had to face different problems contingent to the various phases of the development of production. Some differences in (national or organizational) cultural practices (that is to say, forms of decision making and locus of responsibility) resulted in the crystallization of issues. These issues led to the development of negotiated solutions and, consequently, the development of a specific organizational culture. In brief, they show that organizational culture development is foremost linked to salient issues and their resolution rather than the cultural (national) profile of those (people or organizations) involved in the interaction.

By studying a Danish–Japanese collaboration and addressing the organizational culture and communication level, Clausen (2007) provides another illustration of the negotiated culture perspective. She shows how the terms of the collaboration are negotiated as a function of external constraints and emerging issues linked, for example, to entry barrier, distribution and global brand strategy. The organizational culture that emerges contains aspects of both partners (Danish headquarters and Japanese alliance partner) and, depending upon the negotiated solutions that were found, idiosyncratic new ones as well. In this volume, Lisbeth Clausen pursues another study on corporate communication between Danish and Japanese partners. She shows (see Chapter 7) how various levels of culture can influence the communication process and participate in the emergence of practices through ongoing communication.

Different Forms of Negotiation: Conversation and Reinterpretation

The cases illustrate in this volume several forms of negotiations that lead to the emergence of corporate practices of negotiated culture and intercultural management practices. For example, negotiations take place between organizations, headquarters and subsidiaries, professional groups and individuals. They can touch upon knowledge or technology transfer, strategy and communication, and corporate social responsibility. Three chapters address intercultural issues and how culture develops with negotiated meanings in a way that is different from a direct negotiation between present business partners. Chapter 6 reveals how foreign management practices are reinterpreted in a Tunisian organization, leading to change and new meaning associations. This form of reinterpretation is also addressed in Chapter 5. Chapter 2 shows that the negotiation can take place between a single individual and her environment, with the case of an international consultant who gives a very private meaning to non-places. Chapter 11 reveals that, with the absence of a negotiation partner, meanings are neither developed nor changed and become disconnected from reality. This shows that Western meanings about the 'non-Western' are reproduced in a way that no longer matches the contemporary, complex and multidirectional business reality. They are lacking a reinterpretation.

MEANING SYSTEMS

Since a nation is so diverse that it seems impossible that people may share similar meanings through their diversity (location, religion, age, social group, political affiliation, ethnic group, family status and so on), many interpretive researchers feel reluctant to consider that meanings or sense-making can be linked to the population of a country. However, we know from our experience that similarities do exist between people who grew up in the same country. Currently, the cultural dimension frameworks are useful constructs to point out these similarities. We also know as we demonstrate in the following cases that cultural dimensions are ill-suited for explaining situations of interpersonal interactions (see also Brannen and Salk, 2000; McSweeney, 2009). A few chapters in this volume build upon a stream of research that d'Iribarne (1989) initiated and which uses the alternative notion of meaning systems[4].

Meaning Systems Rather than 'Shared Meanings'

Consider, for example, the following statement: 'Robin Jonsson is competent'. What does competent mean for you? Could it mean that this person possesses the skills to do her job properly: that she is capable and qualified? Could it also mean that you believe this person knows the requirements of the job and can act autonomously? And does it also mean that you will trust this person's analysis of a professional situation and allow her to bypass procedures if she deems it appropriate? Sylvie Chevrier reveals in Chapter 4 the interrelated meanings encompassed in the notion of 'competence', which the French aid workers use in their interactions: the ideas of being capable and qualified, the notion of autonomy, responsibility and awareness of the demands of the job, and a certain degree of granted freedom to interpret rules – not to bend rules, but to interprct them. (This means knowing how and when to best apply them.) All meanings are interlinked with the notion of competence: they form a meaning system.

The meaning system used by the French aid workers echoes the way other French people make sense of competence in a work environment (see Chevrier, 2003; d'Iribarne, 1989, 2006). When similar meaning systems are found across professions, industries, and generations within the same country, we can talk about a (socio-)cultural meaning system. This meaning system has been acquired and is present in the French cultural background. For example, this meaning system may be present in the way the national educational system values competence. This may be displayed in various novels and theatrical plays; it may be an organizing principle in professional trainings; it may even be at the centre of debates in professional organizations and so on.

Does this mean that all French share this meaning system around the notion of competence? Not exactly. This meaning system is probably known to most people socialized with a French cultural background. However, they may disapprove of it and, for example, think that competence and autonomy should not be linked with each other. However, they tend to refer to similar items when discussing competence (that is to say, either supporting or not supporting their association with the idea of competence). In other words, people may have different opinions; however, patterns in the expression of these opinions tend to present striking similarities within national contexts (Chevrier, 2009; d'Iribarne, 2006, 2009). In sum, meaning systems are an articulation of meanings: not shared meanings and certainly not a shared opinion. This stands in clear contrast to previous interpretive studies that have defined and investigated culture as shared meanings, inspired by the works of Geertz (1973) or Berger and Luckmann (1966), for example.

Meaning Systems Help Understand the Role of Culture

Meaning systems can be used to grasp fragments of the culture that members of a group have in common or are developing. Meaning systems are only fragments; they can only reflect a limited cultural aspect, such as a notion or a concept. However, these aspects can have important implications in a given environment. Consider, for example, the importance of the notion of freedom in contemporary America and its implications for both internal and foreign policies. Similarly, the North American notion of ethics is such that an organization can be perceived as an ethical actor, whereas it is not in other national contexts. This leads to interesting situations when the headquarters of North American companies want to transfer their 'codes of conduct' – to Europe, for example (see Chapter 5 by Christoph Barmeyer and Eric Davoine).

Meaning systems do not have the ambition of explicating a culture, as though culture were something stable and monolithic. Conversely, meaning systems reveal how a group of people use interconnected meanings to make sense of past, present or future situations and how they themselves transform the meaning systems they use. For example, Hèla Yousfi claims in Chapter 6 that the metaphor of a family is frequently used in Tunisian organizations, which leads to potential 'dysfunctions' (for example, the absence of explicit rules or favouritism). She demonstrates in her case study of an exceptional Tunisian organization that the family metaphor is also used; however, it is employed with a twist: written rules. The introduction of an 'American' management model (that is to say, performance assessment and job description) did not replace the metaphor of the family. Rather, it consolidated it because it could control its dysfunctions. This meaning system connecting an organization and a family is flexible: it can encompass new meanings, reinforce others and keep its role of sense-making for the employees in the organization.

Knowing which meaning system is used enables us to better understand how people analyse situations, which helps us to work together effectively (see especially Chapter 4). In sum, meaning systems are well matched for the study of interaction; they offer an analysis on the level of interpersonal interaction – the level on which we experience them. They also show the dynamic and changing aspect of cultures.

INTERCULTURAL INTERACTIONS AND POWER ISSUES

With this volume and the cases it presents, we want to stress that we need to address the power balance between the partners in interaction since it affects the way culture and cultural differences are discussed and how meanings are negotiated in interactions.

Talking about Culture (and What it Can Mean)

Studies conducted from an interpretive cross-cultural management perspective have revealed that talking about cultural differences can mean different things to different people (see, for example, Barinaga, 2007; Søderberg and Vaara, 2003; Vaara et al., 2003). This can come in a variety of ways: the depiction of experienced differences as much as a constructed story; a way to organize or separate employees; or as an 'excuse' for explaining a current situation.

For example, Riad (2005) and Vaara (2002) show that organizational or national culture differences can be a narrative construction – a story – to explain the success or the failure of mergers and acquisitions. Common in connection to unsuccessful mergers are such elements as talking about cultural differences, cultural distance, cultural incompatibility or the like. This is a convenient way to silence other analyses that could reveal different issues (such as a poorly prepared merger).

In some cases, people tend to contradict the cultural dimension scores for their country or the one they are describing when they talk about culture and cultural differences. How is this possible? It may be due to local idiosyncrasies or, as Ybema and Byun (2009) argue, talking about cultural differences may also be a way to render the other 'different', especially if they are in another hierarchical position. These boundaries (that is to say, between 'The Dutch' and 'The Japanese') separate employees and perpetuate the reproduction of power and status inequalities in organizations. The authors show that the discourse on culture that employees have held is constructed and mobilized in connection to power inequalities (see also Cohen and El-Sawad, 2007).

Tienari et al. (2005) give a similar example of the association of 'cultural differences' or different nationalities with a situation of inequality. The authors wonder about the lack of females in top management positions at a large Nordic bank; they reveal how the (male) managers in a dominant position use culture and national differences in a discourse that excludes females. Their respective national identities are expressed in a way that distances gender: a focus on females appears irrelevant or out of place, thus implicitly supporting the fact that women are absent from top management positions.

In sum, when interviewees bring cultural differences to the forefront – either by supporting or denying cultural differences – it may indicate an issue of power that will influence the intercultural interaction.

Power (Im)balance in Intercultural Interaction

Interviewees argue in this volume that cultural differences are problematic (see Chapters 4, 5 and 8). Interestingly, the ones who talk about cultural differences appear to be those who need to adapt to the situation. In contrast, other actors present cultural differences as being almost irrelevant (in Chapters 2, 3 and 8). Conversely, those who have this discourse in these cases are the ones who seem to hold positions of power. Additionally, a third configuration appears: the discourse on cultural similarities or the need for cultural adjustment (Chapters 4, 6, 7, 9 and 10). These are the cases when collaboration goes well and is creative: where any power differences seem the most balanced.

Chapter 3 by Sampo Tukiainen illustrates how talking about 'cultural differences' can be a substitute when referring to a power struggle between different national partners in interaction. The tensions expressed by ethnocentrism are linked to a power struggle between individual managers and two forms of knowledge. Finnish engineers have a technological knowledge advantage, while the Polish subsidiary has a local knowledge advantage. This tension is exacerbated by the advantages that are linked to holding a position of leadership in the project (authority, employment and future contracts). In sum, the ethnocentrism that manifested in this project was strongly linked to divergent individual and organizational strategic interests.

Chapter 8 illustrates the strategy of de-emphasis of (national) cultural difference in a power struggle. German engineers resist cross-cultural management training, arguing that they share the professional culture of their colleagues in India. This means that they silence the existing cultural differences that may exist between them and those from India; indeed, they impose a 'German' communication mode between them. Their attitude defies the human resource department (and the non-engineers in general) and is consistent with their view that the organization is best served by engineers. De-emphasizing national differences and emphasizing professional culture help them in maintaining their positions of power. It is not a question of Germans versus Indians: they are all engineers versus non-engineers. But when their position is threatened by the success of the Indian operations, the same engineers suddenly talk about the engineers in India as 'the others', insisting upon their differences.

A discourse on cultural similarity is best illustrated in Chapter 10. Chinese and Brazilian counterparts underline what they have in common (real or invented), working actively on a cultural integration of the joint ventures. It seems that the differences between the partners are well balanced (in terms of know-how, technology, knowledge of the environment and so on); these are also the collaborations that are the most creative. Both partners are shown to have actively adapted to the other and to have grown in this exchange.

Power imbalance is an aspect of the discourse that the interviewees praise. It influences how they will negotiate their differences; thus, it is an issue that needs to be considered in intercultural relationships. People may be less likely to revise their position and consider cultural differences in dominant positions of power. However, people may use the cultural difference discourse in a weak position to resist imposition of one model. Since nations also have a history of interaction, power imbalance can be seen in the general context of the situation. When Vietnamese and French collaborate in a development project, the colonial history of the two countries is implicit and can influence the partners towards false interpretations. When Western European experts come to transfer knowledge and train employees from Bulgaria or Poland, they embody the triumphant West. When a Scandinavian-looking consultant travels through developing countries to promote security or a police solution, he represents the developed West. Necessary for this analysis is perceiving the power imbalance that is part of the situation and of the context(s) of the interaction. And contextual elements can be on a supra-national level as well (as Iris Rittenhofer shows in Chapter 11) with implicit ways 'Westerners' tend to think of others and act in relation to them.

CONCLUSION

We first explained in this chapter what we meant by interpretive cross-cultural management research. We detailed implications on the kind of practical and firsthand knowledge that is developed and how the study of meanings can be performed (for researchers and for practitioners). We explicated the theoretical framework of culture and negotiated meanings, the notion of meaning systems that may be found in a given national context and the necessity to consider power in the intercultural interactions. Equipped with this knowledge, one can make the most of the theoretical, as well as empirical contributions of the next ten case studies, which illustrate cross-cultural management in practice.

NOTES

*   This chapter is part of the research project 'The hidden side of cross-cultural management', financed by Vetenskapsrådet, the Swedish Research Council (421-2009-2020).
1.   Some argue that the centre of interpretive investigation should be the experience of people; others say that we should concentrate on the social artefact (for example, language) that is created by people. A focus on experience is praised by phenomenologists, who stress the life-world (see, for example, Dilthey, Husserl, Schutz). A focus on the artefacts is argued by hermeneuts (for example, Ricœur). Simmel pleads for a focus on both; we do also, as evidenced in this chapter. We invite you to consult Hatch and Yanow (2003) for an introduction to this discussion.
2.   Interpretive research differentiates between different forms of understanding, such as, for example, *Begreifen* and *Verstehen*. Weber argues that grasping (*Begreifen*) a phenomenon means understanding in an external way. This form of understanding is favoured in positivist sciences, aiming at models, laws and the like. Weber insists that the study of human beings should be different, for two main reasons: human beings have meanings associated with their actions, so actions are never totally external to them (as if following laws); second, researchers, as fellow human beings, have the ability to share these meanings and, thus, reach a different form of understanding (*Verstehen*). For example, they can empathize with the people they study and understand (from the inside) the reasons of their actions. We invite you to read Schwandt (1994, 2000) for a further discussion on the different views of V*erstehen*.
3.   We invite you to consult the various editions of *The Sage Handbook of Qualitative Research* edited by N.K. Denzin and Y.S. Lincoln (2005) for details on the different qualitative methods. You can also consult the work of Kvale (1996) on 'InterViews' for an in-depth discussion of qualitative interview techniques and the work by B. Czarniawska (2004), *Narratives in Social Science Research*, to understand the process of narrative analysis.
4.   We use the term 'meaning system' as a translation of the notions of '*cadres de sens*' or '*structure de sens*'. In the cases, authors also refer to 'sense-making systems' (Chapter 4) or 'frames of meanings' (Chapter 6).

REFERENCES

Alvesson, M. and K. Sköldberg (2000), *Reflexive Methodology. New Vistas for Qualitative Research*, London: Sage.

Barinaga, E. (2007), 'Cultural diversity' at work: "national culture" as a discourse organizing an international project group', *Human Relations*, **60**(2), 315–40.

Barkema, H. and F. Vermeulen (1997), 'What differences in the cultural background of partners are detrimental for international joint ventures?', *Journal of International Business Studies*, **28**(4), 845–64.

Berger, P. and T. Luckmann (1966), *The Social Construction of Reality: A Treatise in the Sociology of Knowledge*, London: Penguin Books.

Brannen, M.Y. (2004), 'When Mickey loses face: recontextualization, semantic fit and the semiotics of foreignness', *Academy of Management Review*, **29**(4), 593–616.

Brannen, M.Y. and J. Salk (2000), 'Partnering across borders: negotiating organizational culture in a German-Japanese joint venture', *Human Relations*, **52**(4), 451–87.

Chevrier, S. (2003), *Le Management Interculturel*, Paris: Presses Universitaires de France.

Chevrier, S. (2009), 'Is national culture still relevant to management in a global context? The case of Switzerland', *International Journal of Cross Cultural Management*, **9**(2), 169–84.

Clausen, L. (2007), 'Corporate communication challenges: a "negotiated" culture perspective', *International Journal of Cross-Cultural Management*, **7**(3), 317–32.

Cohen, L. and A. El-Sawad (2007), 'Lived experiences of offshoring: an examination of UK and Indian financial service employees' accounts of themselves and one another', *Human Relations*, **60**(8), 1235–62.

Czarniawska, B. (2004), *Narratives in Social Science Research*, London: Sage.

Denzin, N.K. and Y.S. Lincoln (eds) (2005), *The Sage Handbook of Qualitative Research. Third Edition*, Thousand Oaks, CA: Sage.

d'Iribarne, P. (1989), *La logique de l'honneur*, Paris: Le Seuil.

d'Iribarne, P. (2002), 'Motivating workers in emerging countries: universal tools and local adaptations', *Journal of Organizational Behavior*, **23**(3), 243–56.

d'Iribarne, P. (2006), *L'étrangeté française*, Paris: Le Seuil.

d'Iribarne, P. (2009), 'National cultures and organizations in search of a theory: an interpretative approach', *International Journal of Cross-Cultural Management*, **9**(3), 309–21.

Geertz, C. (1973/1993), *The Interpretation of Cultures*, London: Fontana Press.

Gertsen Cardel, M. and A.-M. Søderberg (2010), 'Expatriate stories about cultural encounters – a narrative approach to cultural learning processes in multinational companies', *Scandinavian Journal of Management*, **26**(3), 248–57.

Guba, E.G. and Y.S. Lincoln (2005), 'Paradigmatic controversies, contradictions and emerging confluences', in N.K. Denzin and Y.S. Lincoln (eds), *The Sage Handbook of Qualitative Research. Third Edition*, Thousand Oaks, CA, Sage, pp. 191–215.

Hatch, M.J. and D. Yanow (2003), 'Organization theory as an interpretive science', in H. Tsoukas and C. Knudsen (eds), *The Oxford Handbook of Organization Theory*, Oxford, Oxford University Press, pp. 63–87.

Hofstede, G. (1980), *Cultures' Consequences: International Differences in Work-related Values,* Beverly Hills, CA: Sage.

Hofstede, G. (2001), *Culture's Consequences: Comparing Values, Behaviors, Institutions and Organizations Across Nations*, 2nd edn, Thousand Oaks, CA: Sage.

House, R.J., P.J. Hanges, M. Javidan, P.W. Dorfman and V. Gupta (eds) (2004), *Culture, Leadership and Organizations: The GLOBE Study of 62 Societies*, Thousand Oaks, CA: Sage.

Irrmann, O. (2008), 'L'analyse interculturelle en gestion: une approche interactionniste', in E. Davel, J.-P. Dupuis and J.-F. Chanlat (eds), *Gestion en contexte interculturel. Approches, problématiques, pratiques et plongées*, Laval, QC, Canada: Presses de l'Université Laval et Télé-université (UQAM), pp. 119–62.

Kirkman, B.L., K.B. Lowe and C.B. Gibson (2006), 'A quarter century of culture's consequences: a review of empirical research incorporating Hofstede's cultural values framework', *Journal of International Business Studies*, **37**(3), 285–320.

Kvale, S. (1996), *InterViews: An Introduction to Qualitative Research Interviewing*, Thousand Oaks, CA: Sage.

McSweeney, B. (2009), 'Dynamic diversity: variety and variation within countries', *Organization Studies*, **30**(9), 933–57.

Nardon, L. and R.M. Steers (2009), 'The culture theory jungle: divergence and convergence in models of national culture', in R.S. Bhagat and R.M. Steers (eds), *Cambridge Handbook of Culture Organizations and Work*, Cambridge: Cambridge University Press, pp. 3–22.

Riad, S. (2005), 'The power of "organizational culture" as a discursive formation in merger integration', *Organization Studies*, **26**(10), 1529–54.

Romani, L. (2010), *Relating to the Other: Paradigm Interplay for Cross-Cultural Management Research*, 2nd edn, Saarbrücken, Germany: LAP Publishing.

Schwandt, T. (1994), 'Constructivist, interpretivist approaches to human inquiry', in N.K. Denzin and Y.S. Lincoln (eds), *Handbook of Qualitative Research*, Thousand Oaks, CA: Sage, pp. 118–37.

Schwandt, T. (2000), 'Three epistemological stances for qualitative enquiry: interpretivism, hermeneutics and social constructivism', in N.K. Denzin and Y.S. Lincoln (eds), *The Handbook of Qualitative Research*, 2nd edn, Thousand Oaks, CA: Sage, pp. 189–213.

Schwartz, S.H. (1994), 'Beyond individualism/collectivism: new cultural dimensions of values', in U. Kim, H.C. Triandis, C. Kagitcibasi, S.-C. Choi and G. Yoon (eds), *Individualism and Collectivism: Theory, Method and Applications*, London: Sage, pp. 85–119.

Søderberg, A.-M. (2006), 'Narrative interviewing and narrative analysis in a study of a cross-border merger', *Management International Review*, **46**(4), 1–20.

Søderberg, A.-M. and E. Vaara (eds) (2003), *Merging Across Borders. People, Cultures and Politics*, Copenhagen: Copenhagen Business School Press.

Strauss, A.L. (1978), *Social Negotiations: Varieties, Contexts, Processes and Social Order*, San Francisco, CA: Jossey-Bass.

Tienari, J., A.-M. Søderberg, C. Holgersson and E. Vaara (2005), 'Narrating gender and national identity: Nordic executives excusing for inequality in a cross border merger context', *Gender, Work and Organization,* **12**(3), 217–47.

Trompenaars, F. (1993), *Riding the Waves of Culture: Understanding Cultural Diversity in Business*, London: Nicholas Brealey Publishing.

Vaara, E. (2002), 'On the discursive construction of success/failure in narratives of post-merger integration', *Organization Studies*, **23**(2), 211–48.

Vaara, E., A. Risberg, A.-M. Søderberg and J. Tienari (2003), 'Nation talk. The construction of national stereotypes in a merging multinational', in A.-M. Søderberg and E. Vaara (eds), *Merging Across Borders. People, Cultures and Politics*, Copenhagen, Denmark, Copenhagen University Press, pp. 61–86.

Ybema, S.B. and H. Byun (2009), 'Cultivating cultural differences in asymmetric power relations', *International Journal of Cross-Cultural Management*, **9**(3), 339–58.

2. On the road again: culturally generic spaces as coping strategies in international consultancy

Sara Louise Muhr and Jeanette Lemmergaard

INTRODUCTION

For a long time, research in cross-cultural management has discussed what culture is and how it can be identified (Sackmann and Phillips, 2004; Yeganeh and Su, 2006), as well as how culture influences management practices (Laurent, 1983) and organizational competitiveness (Redding, 1994). In this way, culture has long been an important part of management studies – both across countries and across organizations within the same country (Mohe, 2008). However, to obtain a deeper understanding of cross-cultural work and its effect on employees we find it important also to examine how employees, who work across cultures, cope with constantly changing working environments. This chapter therefore takes a different approach, as it is about subjective experiences in cross-cultural work.

To do this, we analyse cross-cultural work in the specific situation of an international consultant. Working in constantly changing settings influenced by different organizational and national cultures makes the international consultant a 'temporary worker' (Garsten, 1999), who changes place of work on a continuous basis, and who's sense of belonging is constantly defined and redefined (Fleming and Spicer, 2004). When international consultants operate in many different countries over a short period of time they are constantly surrounded by new people and new cultures. This constant change holds the risk of alienating the consultants and turning them into strangers in their temporary work environments. As argued by Sturdy (1997), the constant travelling and trying to 'fit in' are often experienced as pressure and anxiety – an experience the employees are often left alone with. In this chapter, we wish to show how an international consultant works and lives in this particular form of solitude, where he – despite rarely being alone – is constantly faced with a kind of solitude; that is, the kind of solitude arising from being placed in multiple and constantly changing cultures away from familiarity.

In investigating how the international consultant copes with this challenge of cross-cultural work, we take a critical approach to culture and question the assumption that culture is always dense, present and influential. We argue the opposite and claim that culture is not always dense, present and influential. Some places are more generic regarding culture than others. However, this does not make these places less important in cross-cultural research; in fact we argue that the spaces of generic culture, so-called 'non-places' (for example, airports, conference rooms, cash machines, large supermarkets and so on), provide cross-cultural workers with a sense of familiarity and identity, which they use to cope with working across multiple cultures.

Illustrated through a case study of an international consultant, we show how these non-places are used in cross-cultural identity work. In doing this, we investigate how the familiarity of non-places such as airports, airplanes and international chain hotel rooms are used by the consultant to cope with his extreme work conditions of the international consultant. Hereby, we show how the non-places support the consultant's identity work and create a sense of belonging, whereas these places have been argued to create the opposite (a sense of anonymity and 'solitary contractuality', see Augé, 1995, p. 94). The chapter contributes to the field of cross-cultural management with the argument that spaces of generic culture are important, but overlooked, aspects of understanding cross-cultural work.

METHODOLOGY

The single-case design used for this study is based upon numerous in-depth interviews with a senior consultant of a Scandinavian consultancy company (from now on called Interconsult) as well as document analysis of several of Interconsult's internal documents and publications. Over a period of nine months, several in-depth interviews with the consultant about his work experiences were conducted. Most of the interviews were open-ended and discovery-oriented. Four interviews were semi-structured. These four interviews were taped, transcribed and translated, but many more have taken the form of informal conversations and short probing phone calls. Most of the interviews focused on the consultant's work experiences, working schedule, habits, and the different roles and identities the consultant takes in different projects. Based on these interviews, we investigate how the consultant copes with the form of work and with the foreignness and solitude that goes along with working abroad and across constantly changing multiple cultures. This then leads us to a discussion of how the type of work affects the consultant's sense of belonging, and in the end how this influences not only his work but also his identity work.

CASE STUDY: THE CONSULTANT'S EXPERIENCES

Interconsult, which employs about 100 people, carries out research, offers courses and education, and conducts consultancy and coaching for implementation of national and international projects. As the organization provides both national and international services, it is divided into a national and an international department. Our study focuses on the international department. Most of the consultants in this particular department work from abroad more than half of the time mainly on projects in developing countries. An average project has a duration of 6–18 months and the consultants often work on several projects simultaneously, which means that they travel from one part of the world to another and home again several times during a project. The projects often overlap, which means that the travelling is not concentrated on a 6–18 months period followed by time at the home office. Constantly traveling between home and different project destinations is the typical way of working in the international department of Interconsult.

The consultant, who is the focal point of this study, has been with Interconsult for 15 years and is placed directly under the executive director in the international department. During these years the consultant mainly worked on international projects in – among other places – South Africa, Tanzania, Mozambique, Vietnam, Cambodia, Guatemala, Serbia, Iraq and Afghanistan. These countries are all very different with regard to norms and cultures, and most of the countries are geographically placed at a considerable distance from Scandinavia. All the projects the consultant has worked on were carried out in collaboration with the government or a governmental institution in the client's country. In this way, all the projects were political in nature, that is, working with justice policy, the police, security or legislation issues.

> We often work on several projects at a time, sometimes I find myself having worked on projects in Europe, South Africa, South America, and Asia – all in a few months. But all of the projects have the same model as foundation, that is, the model Interconsult has developed, and that gives them [the projects] some sense of similarity.

In this way, the consultant explains that his work is a mixture of similar concepts and different cultures. Because his work is political in nature and because he works with many different cultures and people with different interests, he often has to be very conscious about how he acts and appears towards other people. Most of the consultant's work depends on being able to understand local contexts and cultures and take on different roles whenever necessary. He mentioned several times during the interviews that he puts a lot of effort into identifying with the clients to better understand their point of views and 'fight their case'. He is personally involved when he is at a project, and therefore he also needs the time travelling as time off.

When I'm traveling, I see the time on the airplane most of all as my 'time off', a time which I can spend as I like. I usually spend the time on my long flights reading or catching up on sleep. When I enter the plane, I switch off mentally; the time on the plane is holy to me. Many of the stewardesses recognize me, and they know what I want. I get a drink and a meal and shortly after, I sleep like a rock. Nothing can wake me up, not bad turbulence, not screaming children, nothing. Sometimes when I wake up, I feel that the other passengers stare at me. I don't know whether it is because I've snored really loud or whether it is because they're amazed I can sleep from it all. Sometimes, I don't even notice that we have landed. And to be honest, I feel sorry for the people traveling with me, because I snore. But I feel at home on the plane, I can rest.

The consultant might use the time on the plane as free time, but when he reaches his destination, he changes. The plane and the destination are two different worlds for him, and he is able to change completely between the two. When he is at his 'free-space' on the plane, he does not bother to talk to anyone. He never chats with the person next to him, and never engages with the people he meets on board the plane. But the minute the plane has landed, he is professional and he is dedicated to the task at hand and the people there.

When I reach my destination I am 'on' from the second I step out of the plane. I am professional and 100 percent dedicated to the project. I feel responsible to my hosts and always go to all the dinners. Usually however, I bring a colleague to take care of the necessary small-talk. I go to all the dinners, but I'm not a small-talker. I discuss business.

The consultant has a very professional approach to business. He takes pride in his professionalism and does not mix business with pleasure. He is very aware of his need to separate his professional and private life, and as much as he loves to be in the job, he tells us that he needs to 'pull the plug' when he is at a 'free place' like on the airplane.

As most of the time he is assigned to projects in developing countries, he has from time to time experienced some pretty rough events, which necessitate an ability to distinguish work life from private life. It becomes very important for him to be able to leave the sphere of work; and if he cannot do that physically, he does it mentally.

Once, I was lying in my hotel room at night. There were shootings – also that night. But this night they did sound very close by. Well, I went to sleep, like I always do, and besides, what else was there to do. I always feel safe at my five star hotel room. The hotel was international ground so to speak. But when I woke up the next morning there were bullet holes in the wall facing the street, and I must admit that shook me a little.

The consultant has numerous examples of similar stories of, for example, fighting, plane crashes, shootings. These incidences do not seem to bother him. In the interviews, he never expressed any feelings of being part of these incidences. He regards himself as a foreigner, who is not involved in the local strifes and fights and in a way protected from the incidences.

> Sometimes, I am picked up directly at the plane and driven in a cortege of bullet-proof black cars. They drive insanely fast, and it all seems very surreal at times.

> It is all so intense that I need to withdraw myself from time to time. That is why I have learned to sleep through almost anything. That is why I can sleep through shootings or terrible turbulence. I need my time to unplug to do this job.

Judging from the stories, it seems as if it is not an option to do his work half-heartedly. He is either 'on' or 'off'. There is no in-between. It is of course due to his unquestionable dedication to the projects. But, as he in the interviews points out himself, it is also due to his physical appearance. He is a physically large person with a very distinct Northern European/Scandinavian look and a deep powerful voice. And he gesticulates heavily; he is noticed – especially in foreign cultures.

> I try to adapt to local customs and cultures, but I cannot change myself, I am what I am. And I am noticed, especially in the African, Asian, and South American countries where I most often travel. I am white as white can be, taller and generally bigger than my clients. There is no doubt about who the foreigner is.

The consultant laughs when he says this. His apparent difference does not seem to be a problem for him, never a liability. It appears as if he most of the time does not think of being especially foreign, instead he disappears into professionalism.

> Already when I ran one of my first projects, something happened to my attitude. When I started to talk about something, I got so caught up in it that I forgot who I was talking to. I talk to the eyes I see, and whether they are placed in a man or a woman or a black or a white doesn't really mean anything to me. And apparently that brought me great luck as I very quickly got the nickname 'color blind'. And it has that important advantage that I quickly take a professional approach and always keep the communication so to speak at an adult level. And that enhances your influence significantly. When the situation is critical and cramped with conflicts, this attitude really pays out. By having this reputation, people rarely question our agenda no matter how delicate the situation becomes, and that gives us a high degree of influence, especially in critical situations.

FOREIGNNESS IN CROSS-CULTURAL WORK

Working for Interconsult, the consultant is constantly subjected to extreme cultural changes. He works most of his time in developing countries where the language, norms and values are very different from a Western conception. In addition, he is engaged in projects that deal with cultural, political and/or legal issues, which means that the work itself is also characterized by strong cultural influences. He tries to understand these foreign cultures he works in, and he has a flair for sensing other cultures and their needs; otherwise he would not be doing what he does. He is noticeably different from the locals, but due to his position as consultant and expert also always in the centre. He is known and noticed but, on the other hand, he is always out of place, not belonging. It is a way of working filled with contradictions: he is constantly at new places, yet always in a similar situation; he is a stranger, yet always at home. It is a way of working where the identity and foreignness – the same and the other – constantly intertwines.

Even though the consultant's working conditions are rather extreme (with more workdays abroad than at home), his working conditions represent the modern way of working; he is not an exception. More and more employees are working on international projects and are on a continuous basis operating in different cultural settings, moving from place to place and from relation to relation, always being the stranger (Vaiman and Lemmergaard, 2007). But how does this way of working affect the consultant's sense of identity? And more generally, how can people working across cultures cope with the constant defining and redefining of self and other in relation to themselves as international workers and as private human beings? As we see from the interviews with the consultant, the consultant wouldn't want his job any other way. He loves his job, but at the same time it consumes him and he needs breaks. He of course seeks refuge when he gets home, but how does he cope when he is away?

Drawing on Augé's (1995) notion of 'non-places', we suggest that one way he copes with foreignness and with always being a stranger is by seeking the recognizability and familiarity of non-places such as airports, restaurants, hotels and conference rooms. In contrast to most research, which typically emphasizes the relation between belongingness and cultural place (Nocker, 2006; Sarup, 1996), we find that this type of international consultant, who travels on a continuous basis, in fact feels a belonging to the non-places, because these places are associated with familiarity.

SPACES OF GENERIC CULTURE

In his analysis of non-places, Augé (1995) deals with how our contemporary world is filled with neutral spaces where culture and identity become transparent. These are what he calls non-places. As examples of non-places the airport, the highway, the hotel room, chain stores and the conference room are obvious. But also less obvious spaces such as sitting in front of the TV or computer could be argued to be non-places. These places give more or less the same feeling all over the world. They are places existing outside historical and cultural frames. 'If a place can be identified as relational, historical and concerned with identity, then a space which cannot be defined as relational, or historical, or concerned with identity will be a non-place' (Augé, 1995, pp. 77–8). In that sense, the non-places are exactly the opposite of what international workers, like the consultant, set out to analyse and work with.

In this sense, non-places are out of the local, specific context. They are universal spaces. No matter where in the world they are placed, they hold similarities. At airports all over the world the passengers meet the same procedures at, for example security, custom or boarding. Despite the local context, supermarkets all over the world hold a great deal of similarity and often hold more or less the same selection of brands supplemented by some local brands. Chains of stores and restaurants are expanding all over the world, looking exactly the same. Similarly, international hotel chains' hotel rooms and conference facilities all look alike. It could even be claimed that they are designed to make the users forget the context or forget where we are; they seem bared of any cultural specificity.

But sometimes the bareness is exactly what makes the traveller feel at home:

> [The non-place] produces effects of recognition. A paradox of non-place: A foreigner lost in a country he does not know (a 'passing stranger') can feel at home there only in the anonymity of motorways, service stations, big stores and or hotel chains. (Augé, 1995, p. 106)

Non-places are refuges for the foreigner to seek – places where it is possible to 'switch off' and disappear. Someone who works all over the world can find repetition and familiarity at these places, comfort at staying at the same hotel, bared of any cultural indication of which country you are in or slipping into a supermarket where one sees the well-known brands, the taste of home.

Much theory stresses that belonging always is connected to a sense of space (Sarup, 1996), and a relation to other people (Nocker, 2006). Our study, however, shows that consultants working across cultures actually feel a great sense of belonging at non-places and in solitude. We argue that belonging is not only longing to be (Bell, 1999) or longing to be accepted (Nocker, 2006), but also longing to 'be off', in fact longing not to be. Back with his family in his home country the consultant belongs, he is himself. But when he travels he becomes someone else and he takes on roles depending on the specific project. He works at places where culture and roles mean everything, and everything he says and does has to be evaluated and thought through in order not to offend local norms and values. He goes out for dinners, eats 'new' traditional dishes, cannot say no to the local wine, meets wives and families, sometimes of very powerful and charismatic people. And he loves this, but it is also what drains him. The experiences the interviewed consultant has when he is working on the projects are often of a very intense nature, and therefore must in some way affect him emotionally. As a strong contrast, the culturally generic non-places do not disturb him, and in a sense he does not have to have an opinion there Therefore, we suggest that employees working across cultures, being constant strangers, in fact use these non-places to cope with the cultural overload they are exposed to.

Also, it seems he protects himself by maintaining to be a foreigner and seek neutrality at the non-places. He feels safe and protected in the non-places. When he is in his hotel room or the bullet-proof car, he feels safe. These are the same all over the world, the same high international standard. He feels untouchable there, because they are 'international spaces' – free zones. No matter how many bullet holes the hotel wall has or how many emergency land-ings he has experienced, he feels safe and protected in these familiar places.

Even though non-places are culturally generic, they are not spaces of no culture. Instead they are spaces of a kind of accepted, pre-negotiated bland culture. In a sense, this type of culture is very much inspired by Western stan-dards, which is exactly why they appear as spaces of generic culture appro-priate (or recognizable) to a large number of travellers, where a certain culture is dominant yet accepted and pre-negotiated. This pre-negotiated bland culture is in line with the Western hyperreality of globalization (see Chapter 11). This is not the same as to say that these spaces are culture-free spaces; rather they represent spaces of generic cultures. The bleakness of planes, airports, hotel rooms and supermarkets can therefore be argued to be a particular reflection of American or Western culture. They are designed so culturally transparent that they seem recognizable, appropriate to and appeal to the broadest possi-ble (travelling) audience. However, the demand for smooth mobility divides people into a travelling elite of people who can benefit from globalization and a less mobile class who cannot (Bauman, 1998). People, like the consultant, who can travel without being slowed down, move through fast track, are serviced on business class, check in to five star hotels and are picked up by anonymous drivers constitute the travelling elite (Peltonen, 2006), whereas the clients he works for often represents the opposite. The consultant – being part of this elite – is never slowed down, as he inhabits the regulated and controlled spaces that keep the surrounding otherness outside:

> Such purified spaces, free of the dirt, contact, noise, disease and the apparent chaos (and insecurity) of the outside, are typified by an aesthetic control of external and internal trimmings and decor that conform to western tastes. (Kothari, 2006, p. 249)

It is in this sense that the culturally generic spaces are pre-negotiated. They are spaces where a Western traveller, like the consultant, can lay cultural differences aside, where cultural differences matter less (for him) and where familiarity is important.

CONCLUSION AND IMPLICATIONS FOR PRACTITIONERS

This chapter has shown that non-places that are perceived to be culturally generic are very important to understand cross-cultural work. In spaces of generic culture, the culture is so broadly defined that it becomes possible for many different people to identify with and belong. Non-places offer the international traveller a break. In this way, belonging and identity are not only produced in relations arising in cultural spaces, but also in solitude in the familiarity of the non-places. Identity continues to be constructed in the interplay between foreign cultural stimuli and familiar and trivial activities.

As this chapter drew on the experiences of one single international consultant, drawing more general conclusions will need more in-depth investigation. We shall therefore conclude this chapter with a call for more research into the meaning of culturally generic spaces for cross-cultural management. It might seem a paradox that culturally generic spaces should have any influence on cross-cultural management. But perhaps it is for this very reason that it is an important topic to engage in. After all, it is often in paradoxes and dilemmas that interesting research is conducted and not in the obvious.

Similarly for practitioners, our chapter has shown that the less obvious might be worth paying more attention to. When employees are sent out to work in other cultures, the focus is normally on how to manage the strange and foreign. This chapter has shown how people working across cultures can use the familiar as coping strategies. This finding is not only important for organizations constructing and designing non-places, but also for people using them. Knowing their importance might optimize both the construction and the use of them in ways that help the cross-cultural worker cope with the stress of cross-cultural work, but perhaps also warns against the sometimes false sense of security they give.

On this note, it is important to realize the strong Western connotation that they hold. This constitutes an ethical dilemma, both for the users and the creators of such spaces. By creating a division between the travelling elite and the 'rest of the world' we send the signal about certain culture's superiority over others (Özkazanc-Pan, 2008). The travelling elite is often constituted of people who are sent out to 'teach' and 'civilize' the rest of the world (see Chapter 11), very much like the consultant in our study. However taking an ethical reflexive stand to this could question whether the division between the elite and the subject is ethically justified (Loacker and Muhr, 2009). Especially considering the environmental challenges our world is facing, can we justify talking about a travelling elite?

With this chapter, we have therefore aimed to do two things. First, we wanted to show how culturally generic spaces are constructed to function as coping mechanisms for cross-cultural workers. With this, we emphasize the fact that also less culturally specific places are of importance to understand cross-cultural management. However, very importantly we also wanted to use this chapter to point to the problems of such behaviour. Something that is important to consider, especially for the users of these spaces. Most travellers probably don't think much about the meaning of the culturally generic spaces. However under the bland surface lies a very specific cultural question, which we believe is an important one to consider: do we by deeming the Western culture bland and culturally generic create an even deeper separation between what is cultural superior and not? It is not our scope here to attempt to answer such a difficult question. However, by voicing it we hope we can initiate the debate.

REFERENCES

Augé, M. (1995), *Non-Places: Introduction to an Anthropology of Supermodernity*, New York: Verso.

Bauman, Z. (1998), *Globalization: The Human Consequences*, New York: Columbia University Press.

Bell, V. (1999), 'Performativity and belonging. An introduction', *Theory, Culture and Society*, **16**(2), 1–10.

Fleming, P. and A. Spicer (2004), '"You can check out anytime, but you can never leave": Spatial boundaries in a high commitment organization', *Human Relations*, **57**(1), 75–94.

Garsten, C. (1999), 'Betwixt and between: temporary employees as liminal subjects in flexible organizations', *Organization Studies*, **20**(4), 601–17.

Kothari, U. (2006), 'Spatial practices and imaginaries: experiences of colonial officers and development professionals', *Singapore Journal of Tropical Geography*, **27**(3), 235–53.

Laurent, A (1983), 'The cultural diversity of western conceptions of management', *International Studies of Management and Organization*, **13**, 75–96.

Loacker, B. and S.L. Muhr (2009), 'How can I become a responsible subject? The perspective of an "ethics of responsiveness"', *Journal of Business Ethics*, **90**(2), 265–77.

Mohe, M. (2008), 'Bridging the cultural gap in management consulting research', *International Journal of Cross-Cultural Management*, **8**(41), 41–57.

Nocker, M.O. (2006), 'A situated imagination: the performance of belonging and ethics in project work', paper presented at EIASM Workshop, Making Projects Critical: Beyond Project Rationality, Manchester Business School.

Özkazanc-Pan, B. (2008), 'International management research meets the "rest of the world"', *Academy of Management Review*, **33**(4), 964–74.

Peltonen, T. (2006), 'Frequent flyer: speed and mobility as effects of organizing', in P. Case, S. Lilley and T. Owen (eds), *The Speed of Organization*, Malmö, Sweden: Liber, pp. 70–87.

Redding, G. (1994), 'Comparative management theory: jungle, zoo or fossil bed?', *Organization Studies*, **15**(3), 323–59.

Sackmann, S.A. and M.E. Phillips (2004), 'Contextual influences on culture research', *International Journal of Cross-Cultural Management*, **4**(3), 370–90.

Sarup, M. (1996), *Identity, Culture, and the Postmodern World*, Edinburgh: Edinburgh University Press.

Sturdy, A. (1997), 'The consultancy process – an insecure business?', *Journal of Management Studies*, **34**(3), 389–413.

Vaiman, V. and J. Lemmergaard (2007), 'Retention of non-traditional workers in professional service firms: a pressing issue for HRM in the 21st century', paper presented at the 22nd Workshop on Strategic Human Resource Management, 19–20 April, Brussels.

Yeganeh, H. and Z. Su (2006), 'Conceptual foundations of cultural management research', *International journal of Cross-Cultural Management*, **6**(3), 361–76.

3. Dynamics of ethnocentrism and ethnorelativism: a case study of Finnish–Polish collaboration

Sampo Tukiainen*

INTRODUCTION

> In the previous [project] ... at the beginning we had this fight between Finns and Poles ... and we tried to make people understand that this is one project, this is one company, and that we are all in the same boat ... And I think we succeeded pretty well ... Of course now with [the consecutive project] we have had to start it all over again ... it's still a fight about what comes from Finland and what comes from Poland, who's the one knowing better how to do it, who should be the leader, and so on. (Finnish project manager)

In cross-cultural collaboration it is common for nationalism and national cultural polarizations to break out between workgroups, splitting them into conflicting subgroups with 'us-versus-them' attitudes, and with the resultant cultural clashes hindering effective teamwork (Adler, 1997; Hofstede, 1980; Schneider and Barsoux, 1997). Concomitantly, 'ethnocentrism' (that is, the belief of one's own culture and worldview being central and superior to others) is bound to become highly salient between the subgroups (Adler, 1997; Cramton and Hinds, 2005).

Yet, contrasting tendencies have also been observed; some groups are able to develop 'ethnorelativism' (that is, understanding, appreciation and adaptation of different worldviews and cultures), leading to the gradual emergence of negotiated working cultures between the workgroups (Brannen and Salk, 2000; Cramton and Hinds, 2005; Earley and Mosakowski, 2000; Salk and Brannen, 2000). Moreover, it is argued that such ethnorelativism extends beyond immediate collaboration, that is, it generalizes and involves other groups representing the same cultures and nationalities, and produces effective work and cooperation in future cross-cultural collaborations (Cramton and Hinds, 2005).

Such arguments on the transferability and generalizability of ethnorelativism, however, contrast with the message conveyed in the opening quote of

29

this chapter. In this quote a Finnish project manager recounts his experiences from two consecutive projects carried out between his Finnish colleagues and Polish counterparts. As can be seen, the thoughts expressed describe the erosion of the ethnorelativism and collaborative spirit developed during the first project by the beginning of the subsequent project.

Inspired by such an apparent contradiction between practice and what is argued in theory, this chapter delves into the world of international engineering projects, examining in detail the dynamics of ethnocentrism and ethnorelativism within a Finnish–Polish project management team. As the apparent displacement of ethnorelativism with increased ethnocentrism takes place right after seemingly fruitful cooperation in a preceding project, the chapter asks: why did ethnorelativism not transfer from the earlier collaboration to the subsequent one, despite that such transfer is proposed in the existing literature?

By answering this question, this chapter extends earlier conceptual and empirical work on developing and maintaining ethnorelativism and negotiated working cultures in cross-cultural collaborations (Brannen and Salk, 2000; Cramton and Hinds, 2005). This chapter also adds to existing research on triggers activating subgroup 'faultlines' (Chrobot-Mason et al., 2009; Lau and Murnighan, 1998) by highlighting specific cultural and affective factors as well as conflicting strategic interests between the two parties, and the role these play in the erosion of ethnorelativism.

From a practical perspective, this chapter also points out that in addition to developing cross-cultural sensitivity, understanding and appreciating relevant cultures, managers should also pay attention to the underlying strategic interests at the individual and organizational levels of the cultural groups in the collaboration. Consequently, these interests should be taken into account when designing the organizational structures and incentive systems supporting the development and maintenance of ethnorelativism and negotiated working cultures.

RESEARCH SETTING AND METHODOLOGY

The two consecutive projects studied in this research (hereafter, first project and second project) were carried out in Poland by a Finnish parent company and its Polish subsidiary during the 2000s.[1] Both of the projects could be considered to be 'large infrastructural engineering projects' as classified by Miller and Lessard (2000).

To answer the research question, open interviews in the spirit of the ethnographic interviewing technique (Spradley, 1979) were employed. This interview methodology and research philosophy was preferred as it was considered to provide an opportunity to let the interviewees talk about their experiences in their own words, to allow multiple perspectives and interpretations of the lived actuality to emerge and to reduce the likelihood of the author imposing his thoughts and hypotheses on the interviewees.

The data was collected by interviewing the Finnish and Polish project managers (two Finns, one Pole), two Finnish project supervisors, the Vice President of the Finnish parent company (a Finn) and the Chief Executive Officer (CEO) of the Polish subsidiary (a Pole). These individuals represent the majority of the key personnel and the managerial board for both projects. Each of the informants was interviewed one to four times, and each interview lasted between one to two hours. The Finns and the Poles were interviewed separately. Altogether, 11 tape-recorded and transcribed interviews (nine Finnish and two Polish), were carried out by the author. In order to gain more understanding on the Polish perspectives and viewpoints, the Polish project manager was contacted for additional interviews several times. However all of these requests were refused. The Polish CEO also became unavailable for further interviews, because he left the company.

For the case description and analysis in the following sections, all the interview data was first coded according to the way the events leading from the first project to the second project were identified and described by the interviewees. Second, based on this coding a case study write-up (Eisenhardt, 1989) depicting the key phases and events in both of the projects was written up by the author. Quotations from the interview data in relation to a specific phase or event in the two projects were included in this write-up. The overall focus in this within-case analysis (Eisenhardt, 1989) was on depicting how the different interviewees described what had happened and how it had happened. Also included were the interviewees' accounts of why something had happened; such expressions often emerged in the interviews without the author specifically probing for them.

In the following section, the case description builds on the case study write-up, highlighting first that ethnorelativism was achieved in the first project. Second, it will be shown that this did not transfer to the second project. Rather, ethnocentrism appeared on both sides during the organizing of the second project. This will be followed by a more detailed description of the events and sentiments (as described by the interviewees) during the organizing phase for the second project when ethnocentrism increased and replaced the ethnorelativism from the first project.

In the concluding section of the chapter, this case description serves as a basis for the analysis of the reasons preventing ethnorelativism from transferring across the two projects, as well as for the theoretical and practical conclusions.

CASE DESCRIPTION

Signs of Ethnorelativism in the First Project

The following excerpts from the first project illustrate that ethnorelativism between the Finnish and the Polish nationals was achieved during the project:

> ... at the beginning [of the first project] we had this fight between the Finns and the Poles ... and we tried to make people understand that this is one project, this is one company, and that we are all in the same boat, and we're doing one project, and that there should be one common outcome and things like that, so that we could make cooperation and mutual understanding work. And I think we succeeded pretty well. (Finnish project manager)

> During the execution phase of [the first project] I think we succeeded in creating pretty much what you could call a unified team. (Polish project manager).

These excerpts reflect the experiences that the interviewed managers on both sides described with regards to the first project: initial ethnocentrism and disputes between the Finns and the Poles, a split of the project organization into two camps, yet followed by times of gradual rapprochement and increase in cooperation.

Furthermore:

> So without a facilitator ... we would probably have failed, because we could even see in the management that one side was representing one nation and the other side the other ... when they met for the first time for two or three days in a remote place, they realized that both sides really represent professionalism. So they started to respect each other and it was very important ... they understood that the only way is to look for cooperation, consensus, and respect on both sides. (Polish CEO)

> Many times after a problematic situation or meeting I had to meet with our Finnish supervisors and we had to discuss these matters. We discussed that when people come from different backgrounds, we just have to accept and understand that there are multiple ways of reaching a certain milestone. It can't be that ours would be the one and only way. (Finnish project manager)

> I think it's ok to think like [the Polish project managers] thought, we just couldn't understand it like that at first. [The Polish project managers] thought that the contracts we make with the subcontractors have more effects than just this one project ... this is just part of the soft issues that a new contractor has to learn. (Finnish project manager)

Thus, various forms of ethnorelativism (see Hammer et al., 2003) were achieved during the first project, although the project had initially been characterized by ethnocentrism between the two partners.

Signs of Ethnocentrism in the Second Project

The following experiences were then discussed by the same managers with regard to the early phases of the subsequent second project:

> What I have tried to describe here is that during the first project we learned to cooperate pretty well, but once again, when the second project was about to start, there were signs of [the Finns and the Poles] splitting apart, pulling strings in opposite directions and trying to dominate the project. (Finnish project manager)

> ... [in the second project] we had a very similar situation as in the first project, you know – about who should take the top position, [a Finn or a Pole?] ... Yeah, you are right, we had the problem, you know, who should be in the top position, and at that time I strongly said: 'No, now is the time to have a Pole.' (Polish CEO).

Hence, during the early phases of the second project, ethnocentrism once again became highly salient.

In the following section events leading to this situation and further evidence of the increased ethnocentrism are examined in more detail.

Organizing the Second Project

Based on the interviews it became evident that the second project had been under development for many years, and that it was the first implementation of a technological innovation made by the Finnish parent company. It also became evident that initially the project had been designed to be carried out by a project organization divided according to the operations in Poland and in Finland, and staffed extensively by the Finnish workforce. Yet, this kind of planning seemed to ignite a series of disagreements between the two parties. As explained by the Finnish Vice President:

> Then we had to think about the dual-headed management model that would be there ... and we really thought about how to combine this, because we considered that [the Finnish project manager] has to be there so that we can take care of the technology and all the stuff that's related to the Finnish project execution model. And then we saw [the Polish project manager] as a specialist in Poland, with the Polish organization and operations, so both had clear roles and strengths ... But then we had these disagreements ... we thought about what was good if we have [the Finnish project manager] as a project director ... Then one perspective was that a Pole has to have customer responsibility because of the language and culture.

In this situation both parties favoured their own candidates as the overall project director. For example, the Polish CEO described his stance in the following way:

At the time I was completely against having a Finn as a project director, because we knew that most of the activities are in Poland, we already knew that we have experienced, tested people, and the customer was different to [that in the first project]. This customer was very sensitive about making [our company] operations in Poland as real Polish ones.

Holding a contrary perspective, the Finns considered the situation quite differently:

... we discussed how to manage the customer, how [the Finns] have managed customers in different projects, and we said that 'a Finn has been able to work with a Polish customer before, hasn't he?'... [the Polish project manager] was appreciated with regard to taking care of the Polish side ... but to manage this really technological, really advanced project ... because it's a first project of its kind, we wanted to have a senior person who is very experienced and understands the Finnish project culture, and we saw [the Finnish project manager] as that. (Finnish Vice President)

Eventually these disagreements did not only limit to the decision regarding the overall project director, they also encompassed the whole project organization and the division of work and responsibilities between the two parties.

Sources of the Reappearing Ethnocentrism

When describing these disagreements, the interviewees also expressed thoughts and interpretations with regard to the situation, opening the lid for sources of reappearing ethnocentrism.

As already implied, the Finns admitted that:

If we think that it's a whole new type of technology that we haven't delivered anywhere before ... so we wanted to keep it in our hands, at least the technology ... I guess it could also be some sort of jealousy ... We were thinking like, 'since we are the technology provider, shouldn't we be in charge of the project, especially because it's the first time that the technology is used'. (Finnish project manager)

Thus, in this situation, the Finns identified themselves strongly as the developer of the new technology, expressing concerns over the complexity of the new project, and over the required competencies needed for its successful delivery. Obviously, in this respect they felt superior to the Poles.

Taking a contrary position, the Poles emphasized the need to understand the local market and especially the local customer. In this respect the Poles naturally saw themselves superior to the Finns:

... and this customer was a different customer to [the first project]. This customer was very, very sensitive about making [our company] operations in Poland real

Polish ones ... Being the manager of a company ... you have to look at the available resources, best resources first. That must be the first criteria. So nationality was not a criteria, but if I have two equal [project manager candidates], and maybe one is younger and highly acceptable to this customer.

These quotes highlight how the properties of the new project became a source of ethnocentrism, while turning the organizational and national cultural features both to valid arguments and excuses for justifying the stances of the two parties.

In addition, the interviews reveal other highly fundamental factors contributing to the stances of the two parties. First, the partners were clearly driven by very similar yet divergent strategic interests at an organizational level. As described by the Polish CEO:

What I think is that the Finns just might be afraid of losing their jobs to us. I've heard it elsewhere too. They just might feel threatened by [the Poles], because at that time it was clearly stated that the [importance of the] Polish subsidiary and market will grow.

This comment highlights the fact that despite that the Finnish parent company's operations originated from a community with a rich and successful industrial heritage, today the community struggles to maintain previous employment levels as well as its business and industrial attractiveness. From this perspective, the management of the Finnish parent company had a great interest in securing the positions of the Finns in the second project.

On the other hand, the situation was also clearly similar in Poland. As pointed out by the Finnish project manager, reflecting on his experiences from the first project which had been delivered near to the town where the second project was located:

... but this financially unstable company was a local company in the town where we were working on [the first project]. And this town was like many other Polish towns, where they had cut down industry and closed firms, and there's lots of unemployed.

Accordingly, maintaining the levels of employment and developing the Polish workforce was also important to the Polish management. This was stressed by the Polish CEO:

... [The Polish subsidiary] is a mature company with really good and experienced people, and [the second project] is the last chance to change the approach to the selection of key personnel for project teams. Nationality must not have priority because Polish specialists will lose their motivation for further developments and initiatives, and they will never overcome the role of assistants.

Therefore, from the two companies' perspective, the new project was strategically important. Consequently, reappearing ethnocentrism and its associated arguments were clearly an excuse for advancing these strategic interests.

The partners were also driven by highly similar, yet divergent business interests at an individual manager's level. For example, a Finnish project manager stressed that:

> There are two companies involved, both with their own management whose responsibility is to make good profit ... So both managements have their incentives based on their own units' financial performance ... and it's also always nice to be interviewed by the local business press, when things are going well, and then it's this project which generates those profits and turnover; either there or here.

Consequently, the second project was strategically important from the individual manager's perspective. The disagreements clearly resulted from individual power plays, making the reappearance of ethnocentrism an excuse for advancing these interests.

Conclusion of the Negotiations

Eventually, after almost a year-long period of negotiations, a decision was reached according to which the project would be organized based on the principle of a single responsible party. More specifically, the project was to be led by the Poles and the project organization staffed extensively by Polish managers and workforce. This decision was reached by the parties involved under circumstances whereby the Poles' influence had increased due to changes in personnel within the management.

DISCUSSION AND CONCLUSION

The empirical evidence presented above illustrates that despite the ethnorelativism achieved in the first project, this was overridden by ethnocentrism in the second project. It also illustrates that in this situation the reappearing ethnocentrism became a highly multifaceted phenomenon caused by various underlying factors.

Cultural Factors

The properties of the second project clearly increased the salience of cultural factors at different levels, leading to the reappearance of ethnocentrism. That is, because this was to be the first application of a significant new technological innovation, from the Polish perspective an understanding of the Polish market, the customer and Polish culture was deemed to be important. In this respect the Poles' superiority, and their concerns over the Finns' capabilities in understanding the Polish national culture were valid. Similarly, but from the Finns' perspective, as the developer of the technological innovation, understanding the technology as well as the project management model and culture was salient. Consequently, the Finns' perceived technological and project managerial superiority and their concerns over the Poles' capabilities in this respect were also valid.

Affective Factors

Reappearing ethnocentrism was also clearly caused by jealousy over the new, innovative project. For example, as one of the Finnish project managers admitted above, their demands over the control of the second project could indeed be seen as such. It is also easy to imagine these feelings appearing on the Polish side because, according to some of the Finnish interviewees, the Polish CEO especially had had a considerable impact on getting the project awarded in the first place. However, from this perspective, the increased ethnocentrism and the perceived in-group superiority and out-group inferiority were convenient excuses for covering up attempts to control the project for affective reasons rather than a genuine manifestation of cultural concerns.

Organizational and Managerial Factors

On the other hand, the second project was also a 'resource' needed for advancing organizational interests. As previously stated, the Finnish parent company originates from a historical, yet struggling community in terms of its business and industrial attractiveness. In Poland there were also areas struggling economically and socially, particularly in this industry. Therefore, from this perspective, both parties had a similar but divergent strategic interest in the second project to use it to contribute to the profitability of the two business units and to maintain their significance and employment levels.

In a similar vein, the second project was also a 'resource' needed to advance the interests of individual managers. As pointed out above, the second project was to be a joint venture carried out as a cooperation of two independent business units, where the respective managers had their own managerial incentives and targets. Thus, each of the individual managers clearly had an interest to secure the leading positions in the second project, and use this to fulfil their individual managerial interests.

From these two interrelated perspectives, increased ethnocentrism was then more of an excuse to cover up the vested organizational and managerial interests, and the ensuing power plays, rather than a genuine manifestation of the cultural concerns at play.

Theoretical Contributions

Taken together these insights then challenge the conceptual proposition made by Cramton and Hinds (2005), according to which ethnorelativism between cultural groups should generalize and extend from one instance of collaboration to another. Consequently, it is argued here that this is not simply a case of learning to understand and appreciate different cultures and extend that learning to future collaborations. Instead, the potential to extend ethnorelativism can be affected by the properties of the task and the managerial and organizational interests present in the new collaboration. As shown here, during the reorganization for the second project the unique properties of this project and the related organizational and managerial interests all increased in salience. In this situation ethnocentrism then (re)appeared both as a valid argument in terms of cultural differences and partner capabilities, as well as an excuse for covering up the affective factors and organizational and managerial power plays at hand.

In addition, this chapter answers the plea from Brannen and Salk (2000) to extend contextually and temporally the research on shared, negotiated working cultures in international collaborative ventures. More specifically, this chapter extends this literature by illustrating how negotiated working cultures can come apart as well as how they may not be a stable state of affairs, persisting automatically without any repercussions to more conflict-prone phases of collaboration. The chapter also adds to the research on events triggering subgroup 'faultlines' and ethnocentrism (Chrobot-Mason et al., 2009; Lau and Murnighan, 1998) by specifying the roles of affective factors and conflicting organizational and managerial interests in the increase of ethnocentrism and the displacement of ethnorelativism.

Practical Contributions

The findings presented above also point to a significant suggestion for practitioners. As shown, increased ethnocentrism and the displacement of ethnorelativism can involve, on the one hand, cultural factors at different levels (Sackmann and Phillips, 2004) and, on the other hand, affective and political factors (Vaara, 2000 and Chapter 1). Furthermore, it is important for managers to distinguish between these factors as they have significant implications to the orientation of actions when attempting to maintain ethnorelativism between collaborative ventures. That is, in the former case where ethnocentrism springs from cultural factors, managers should direct their actions to increasing the cross-cultural knowledge, acceptance and sensitivity of the parties involved (cf. Earley and Ang, 2003). On the other hand, in the latter situation where ethnocentrism springs from the affective reasons and organi-

zational politicking, managers should direct actions towards developing organizational structures and incentive systems that lessen the urge of the parties
involved to engage in advancing subjective interests. For example, in a situation like the one described here, managers could set up an 'independent' joint
venture project organization to carry out project management and execution,
where both parties own an equal share of this new organization.

NOTES

*   This research has been funded by TEKES (the Finnish Funding Agency for Technology and
     Innovation), the Academy of Finland, the participating company and with grants from the
     Helsinki School of Economics Foundation, the Foundation for Economic Education and the
     Jenny and Antti Wihuri Foundation.
1.   To protect the identity of the company, the author has agreed not to disclose any specific
     details on the projects such as the project type, size, names of the partners and so on. The case
     description in this chapter has been sent for approval by the company's representatives, and
     received their acceptance.

REFERENCES

Adler, N.J. (1997), *International Dimensions of Organizational Behavior*, 3rd edn,
    Cincinnati, OH: South-Western College Publishing.
Brannen, M.Y. and J.E. Salk (2000), 'Partnering across borders: negotiating organiza-
    tional culture in a German-Japanese joint venture', *Human Relations*, **53**(4),
    451–87.
Chrobot-Mason, D., M.N. Ruderman, T.J. Weber and C. Ernst (2009), 'The challenge
    of leading on unstable ground: triggers that activate social identity faultlines',
    Human Relations, **62**(11), 1763–94.
Cramton, C.D. and P.J. Hinds (2005), 'Subgroup dynamics in internationally distrib-
    uted teams: ethnocentrism or cross-national learning?', *Research in Organizational
    Behavior*, **26**, 231–63.
Earley, P.C. and S. Ang (2003), *Cultural Intelligence: Individual Interactions Across
    Cultures*, Stanford, CA: Stanford University Press.
Earley, P.C. and E. Mosakowski (2000), 'Creating hybrid team cultures: an empirical
    test of transnational team functioning', *Academy of Management Journal*, **43**(1),
    26–49.
Eisenhardt, K.M. (1989), 'Building theories from case study research', *Academy of
    Management Review*, **14**(4), 523–50.
Hammer, M.R., M.J. Bennett and R. Wiseman (2003), 'Measuring intercultural sensi-
    tivity: the intercultural development inventory', *International Journal of
    Intercultural Relations*, **27**(4), 421–43.
Hofstede, G. (1980), *Culture's Consequences: International Differences in Work-
    related Values*, Beverly Hills, CA: Sage.
Lau, D.C. and J.K. Murnighan (1998), 'Demographic diversity and faultlines: the
    compositional dynamics of organizational groups', *Academy of Management
    Review*, **23**(2), 325–40.

Miller, R. and D. Lessard (2000), *The Strategic Management of Large Engineering Projects: Shaping Institutions, Risks and Governance*, Cambridge, MA: MIT Press.

Sackmann, S.A. and M.E. Phillips (2004), 'Contextual influences on culture research – shifting assumptions for new workplace realities', *International Journal of Cross-Cultural Management*, **4**(3), 370–90.

Salk, J.E. and M.Y. Brannen (2000), 'National culture, networks, and individual influence in a multinational management team', *Academy of Management Journal*, **43**(2), 191–202.

Schneider, S.C. and J.-L. Barsoux (1997), *Managing Across Cultures*, London: Prentice Hall.

Spradley, J.P. (1979), *The Ethnographic Interview*, New York: Holt, Rinehart and Winston.

Vaara, E. (2000), 'Constructions of cultural differences in post-merger change processes: a sensemaking perspective of Finnish-Swedish cases', *Management*, **3**(3), 81–110.

4. Exploring the cultural context of Franco–Vietnamese development projects: using an interpretative approach to improve the cooperation process

Sylvie Chevrier

INTRODUCTION

When considering development projects, it is generally admitted that imported practices should be adapted to the local context, even though actors in the field are often lacking the appropriate methodology to do this. The adjustment process usually focuses on the cultural context of the 'beneficiaries', that is, the target population. For example, in health care, practitioners are aware that any prevention campaign is useless unless the prescribed behaviours are legitimate in the actors' socio-cultural sense-making system. However, the way the partners, both from the North and the South, adapt to one another in project management processes is neglected. How can the main actors cooperate in a project when they do not share the same conceptions of collective action?

Analysing the cultural differences affecting project management sheds light on the tensions or misunderstandings that occur between actors. Previous research has shown that multicultural teams empirically negotiate their work process drawing upon the various cultural attributes of the team members (Brannen and Salk, 2000). DiStefano and Maznevski (2000) propose a three-step approach to overcome differences and to set up management practices that fit the context. The first and second steps consist in mapping cultural differences and in making them explicit. The last step aims at integrating the different views and developing solutions that may solve any disagreements that occur.

To illustrate the cross-cultural challenges in development projects and provide an example of cultural bridging, this chapter presents the case of the Franco–Vietnamese cooperation in projects managed in Vietnam by a French non-governmental organization (GRET). The first section briefly identifies a few problematic issues in the cross-cultural relationships and the second section explains them by showing how French and Vietnamese partners differ in their relation to work and the social environment. The last two sections analyse the implications of these cultural divergences and propose some clues to help practitioners in their cross-cultural interactions.

CASE PRESENTATION: FRANCO–VIETNAMESE DEVELOPMENT PROJECTS

Several projects are managed by the GRET in Vietnam. The most important aims at setting up collective services to farmers (seed production and selling, fish breeding, animal insurance for stockbreeders). A second project is designed to reduce chronic malnutrition by creating production sites and distribution networks of quality infant food, resulting in products that are cheaper than the imported ones. A third concerns micro-finance. All the projects involve French and Vietnamese workers. The following case study explores the cross-cultural issues of this cooperation and proposes recommendations with regard to such collaboration.

The case study draws upon d'Iribarne's interpretative approach of cultures (2009, pp. 314–16). 'Culture' refers to a stable framework for sense-making that is rooted in a basic fear, widely shared by all members of a society. This threat, as well as the desire to escape it, frequently appears in the vocabulary and expressions of people socialized in a given culture. The examination of the recurrence of preoccupations and specific wordings of a group, when compared with other groups, allows one to reveal its underlying cultural framework.

To grasp national cultures and discover the partners' sense-making systems, it's necessary to understand to what extent actors involved in different projects diverge or converge on the appropriate way to manage collective action. The point is to focus on the different issues that generate problems in the cooperation process, to understand the framework that gives them meaning in each culture and to compare them. Interviews were conducted in 2006 with 40 people involved in the projects. Participants were asked to explain their contribution to the projects, give their opinion on the cooperation process, point out critical incidents and highlight the main strengths and weaknesses of the collaboration process. Conceptions that underpinned project management practices and created tensions in the cooperation process have been identified. Due to limited space, only a few of the differences that make sense of important dysfunctions in projects are presented here.

COOPERATION DIFFICULTIES SEEN THROUGH THE ACTORS' EYES

This section presents some mutual criticisms and some critical incidents mentioned by the interviewees, which actually appeared to be related to cross-cultural differences.

In the interviews, the Vietnamese partners in charge of implementing development projects mainly blamed their French counterparts for two things. First, a lack of understanding of the Vietnamese context and, in particular, the mimicking of practices that may be efficient in other places but not necessarily in Vietnam: 'One cannot transplant here what is effective in Laos, it's not the same thing' (V). The second complaint targets French people who do not spend enough time in the field: 'The technical assistant [TA] must work in the field but in fact, the TA works too much in his office' (V).[1]

However these complaints were greatly outnumbered by the very positive comments relying precisely on the close relations many French partners had with people working in the field.

The French respondents mentioned certain deviations that occurred in some of the projects; for example, micro-finance programmes that benefited the family or the project manager's close relations instead of the initial target population. They decided on the necessity of strict control procedures and close project follow-up.

Other French interviewees regretted local Vietnamese partners' lack of initiative: 'They rely on me and my assistant while it should be their initiative' (F). 'They found it was interesting but they didn't act on their own initiative' (F).

Some of these French respondents who would have liked to support the local teams even, on occasion, took over the leadership of the process from their partners.

Lastly, several critical incidents were reported about some Vietnamese partners' positions that changed radically between face-to-face interactions and public situations. One of the French participants felt betrayed by his partner when the latter changed his mind in a meeting, compared with what they had earlier agreed upon.

> We had prepared the team meeting together in the office before going to the meetings and presenting what we had decided on. In some of the meetings, when he discovered the researchers [from the Ministry of Agriculture] did not agree, he changed his mind. He and his Vietnamese team were all against me whereas we had been in agreement before! (F)

Another French respondent criticizes his Vietnamese superior for changing his discourse according to the circumstances. 'When I see my director in a meeting with another director, he says things that are completely different from what he tells us in the car while driving back to the office' (F).

CASE ANALYSIS: DIFFERENCES IN FRENCH AND VIETNAMESE CULTURES

Examining both partners' cultural sense-making systems helps to understand the previous incidents and constitutes the first step to surmounting them. In this section, the opposed cultural views concerning two issues are compared: (1) the French approach to individual autonomy and the Vietnamese representation of social networks and (2) respective work ethic representations.

Individual Autonomy Versus Social Network

The French context knows a sense-making system interweaving role definition and individual autonomy. Each individual is supposed to develop their own thoughts and convictions and to defend them: this is how they demonstrate their intellectual autonomy. In the work environment, this individual autonomy is delimited by the worker's role definition. However, everyone feels free to interpret their professional duties in their own way (d'Iribarne, 1989). Indeed the French interviewees defined their mission in quite personal ways. 'I invented and redefined my responsibilities with [x] as the project was going on and as we faced constraints' (F).

Each individual gets a position in the social system according to their role and status but remains autonomous to interpret the dos and don'ts attached to the job. Public and private lives have clear-cut borders, professional duties are defined by each occupation tradition.

Conversely in Vietnam, a prevailing sense-making system intertwines social rank and obligations. Each Vietnamese worker is inserted in a social world with clear hierarchies, which create towards the others obligations that go beyond the prescribed tasks. Social rules first impose finding the right way to address people, which implies knowing the protagonists' social situation. For instance, even if there are words in Vietnamese to say 'Mr' and 'Mrs' (*Ong* and *Bà*), they are only used in official situations and reserved for high status people such as local authorities. In most other situations, the terms used mean uncle, aunt, elder brother or sister, younger brother or sister; the speaker finds out what the appropriate form of address is, from the person's age and status.

Furthermore, social positions rule what one must or must not say. For example, one may not question overtly the opinion of a person in a higher position without being extremely careful of one's formulation. Generally speaking, contradicting other people is very delicate especially when one is in a weaker power position. Such a social obligation to avoid confrontation in an unbalanced relationship may explain why some Vietnamese partners changed their minds between the face-to-face interactions and the plenary meetings.

In the French context, using the sense-making system linking role and intellectual autonomy, it is expected that people should be brave and stand up for their convictions, even when faced with strong opposition. In consequence, such a change of mind (as described in the interview) is perceived at best as a lack of coherence and at worst as cowardliness or even betrayal.

Social inclusion also depends on the family and groups to which one belongs. Family ties and group membership create strong obligations between members while obligations are much looser with strangers. This contributes to highlight some deviations in micro-finance programmes that have been identified lately, in which resources were primarily distributed to people close to the project managers. In a Vietnamese environment, it is harder to refuse demands from relatives or friends. Being faithful to the project principles is fundamental for French actors but may be conflicting with loyalty towards one's social group in the Vietnamese context.

Work Ethics

The French respondents feel they have a kind of mission to fulfil, and this mission gives meaning to action beyond formal job descriptions. The specific cooperation for the development context certainly emphasizes the feeling of being vested with a mission. For them, the point is not so much to carry out tasks but rather to commit oneself and to work in a development programme 'spirit'.

To fulfil one's mission, everyone must 'shoulder their responsibilities'. This motto is closely related to the perceived culturally appropriate way to accomplish one's work. Obviously, French people are not the only ones having a sense of responsibility, but the French specificities lie in the definition of what the responsibilities are. In their view, task description is indicative rather than definitive. It constitutes a reference that should be resorted to in case of disagreement but is generally considered as a starting point, an input that is to be interpreted. 'Question: What does "the responsibility of the project" mean? Respondent: There is the implicit meaning and the meaning I gave to it, which are two quite different things' (F).

The French define their work by referring, explicitly or implicitly, to the role that the tradition of the profession associates with their job or function. This image determines what may or may not be done, what should be done, the initiative that must be taken, the rules of the art that are to be followed strictly and conversely the situations in which one can deviate from the rules to achieve greater efficiency.

In the French sense-making system, autonomy in the definition of one's sphere of responsibility goes with autonomy in realizing the job. To be responsible for something does not mean implementing scrupulously a work plan but rather deciding on the appropriate actions according to the circumstances. This implies that trusted workers should not be too closely supervised. In other words, in line with this sense-making system, the ideal is to have a clear framework (general guidelines, objectives, a broad mission) and freedom to act within this framework. In accordance with this French conception of responsibility and autonomy, managers have to leave their teams free to decide how they want to accomplish their tasks, so that they can adapt their activity to local conditions. Thus, assigning a general mission and empowering workers is conceived as the right way to improve team members' sense of responsibility. '[I had to] give the local team a sense of responsibility for the implementation methods. My role was to provide people in the field with good conditions so that they could do their work' (F).

For the French partners, the point is to communicate the goal and the meaning of the action to the teams to enable them to find the appropriate solutions; task descriptions cannot encompass or deal with all possible situations. '[One must] make people adhere to the project and not to impose procedures, make them understand the process. It's because the problems are understood that they can be solved outside the framework of the procedure' (F). 'I used to send very long mails not to detail what was to be done, but [rather] what was to be taken into account or to be understood, so that the person concerned faced with a situation could make the right decisions' (F).

According to French managers, such management practices foster initiatives. Employees may demonstrate their skills and creativity as long as they are not compelled to strictly follow procedures or to literally implement a predefined programme.

French managers who mobilize this sense-making system when managing employees or working with partners aim at agreeing on general guidelines for action and dispatching main responsibilities. After which they expect that empowered actors work according to their own sense of responsibilities within this general framework. In line with the French sense-making system interweaving role and intellectual autonomy, overly detailed instructions may be interpreted as a lack of consideration for or confidence in the employee. When a manager deals with responsible people, they should not have to lead them by the hand or explain in a very detailed manner what is to be done.

In the Vietnamese context, the main conception of work is not as a broad mission to fulfil. The respondents rather see their work as consisting of doing well-defined tasks in order to reach precise objectives. Employees expect detailed instructions from their manager or partners and a close support including defining action plans together. '[What I expect from a manager] is support in the working method' (V). 'We are side by side like two partners. To make up the team, get feedback information, think about how work is going on' (V).

Obviously, the spontaneous French way of treating partners with dignity, which consists in defining broad action frames and letting actors work as they think best, without meddling in their business, may create misunderstandings. For the system of meanings used by the French, such management practices plainly respect responsible employees' professional autonomy. In the system of meanings used by the Vietnamese, these good intentions may be interpreted as the will to place oneself in the decision maker's position and to not collaborate in the execution, which makes them feel like 'assistants' rather than partners. For the French, the manager's role is limited to defining the basic framework and to letting competent people do the work autonomously, but the Vietnamese expect close support and continuous exchanges about the details of the work. They eventually think that French people seek to keep strategic decision making for themselves while the implementation should be kept in Vietnamese hands. 'Distant Northern support (Northern methodology) and a Southern workforce are unlikely to work well. ... If the support is distant, the objectives are well-known but are not achieved' (V). 'If we are to cooperate well, we have to talk together. I refuse distant cooperation; someone in Paris, who comes and visits us on a common project, the benefits are very limited. The Vietnamese side has nothing to learn, it is not interesting'(V).

As stated earlier, other Vietnamese also criticize technical assistants who work too much in their office and not enough in the field. Reciprocally, without detailed guidelines or close support, projects do not go as fast as the French would like, and they complain about the Vietnamese co-workers' lack of initiative. In other cases, the granted autonomy is not used to pursue the expected results, those inherent to the fixed general principles. 'We had empowered the team and expected results! When we discovered that reality was quite different from the principles we had advocated, we tried to increase control' (F).

Work ethics also rely on the definition of competences. From the Vietnamese point of view, competency mainly encompasses technical know-how, that is, knowing how to implement a method or how to use a data processing tool. Increasing their skills is one of the main expectancies of the Vietnamese partners about the cooperation and one of their main motivations for taking part in cooperation projects.

In the French context, competency means knowing the working processes but, as stated earlier, it also implies knowing the demands of the job. The rules of the art guide action and make up references to appraise the work quality. 'Let each one say what he has to say according to the demands of his job in his domain' (F).

As long as workers master their jobs and understand the professional rules, they may be autonomous, which means they are not obliged to blindly follow the procedures, thus leading to the possibility of greater efficiency. In the French view, procedures are instruments but certainly not ends. One should never forget the end objectives. 'At best, the procedure deals with the ideal case, it does not fit every situation. We may bypass the procedure and study each case in particular. We should not forget the real end, the ethics, the values for which we should find the right means' (F).

This particular conception of competency is not shared by the Vietnamese partners and the French sometimes criticize the local actors who do not 'internalize the rules' of the job: 'These agents, who were put at our disposal by the bank [for the project], did not internalize the rules. They did not understand the reason for their work' (F).

DISCUSSION FOR CROSS-CULTURAL MANAGEMENT: TOWARDS VALUING CULTURAL DIVERSITY

The difference in conceptions of 'the right way' to work together is more or less clear for the actors. As they get to know one another, they empirically note differences and make endeavours to cope with them or even make the most out of them. In the next section, some cross-cultural adjustments are presented as well as how protagonists use cultural diversity to speed up projects. The last section proposes some thoughts to help actors to go beyond empirical learning, which depends on each person's sensitivity and experience, and to improve cultural diversity management in the Franco–Vietnamese cooperation for development.

Cross-Cultural Learning

Without any special device to manage the cross-cultural dimension, actors empirically learn and adjust to their counterparts. For instance, French expatriates have learned, following the Vietnamese example, to find solutions to tricky negotiations outside formal meetings, understanding the differentiation between front stage and back stage in the social interactions: 'In official negotiation meetings, nothing is really negotiated, it is done before or afterwards, but not during the planned meetings … During official meetings, it's only set language. Never be in direct confrontation' (F). 'When it's a tricky matter, you must have informal contacts outside formal meetings where decisions are not made' (F).

Another adjustment example concerns an expatriate who speaks Vietnamese and has been in Vietnam for several years. He advocates cooperation practices that seem to particularly fit the specific local context. For instance, he suggests one should be present in the field to collaborate, and this echoes the Vietnamese partners' desires to get closer support: 'Training by accompanying people in the field may be less visible than formal seminars and less efficient compared with the time devoted to it but I think it's very important' (F). 'When we work together, we learn from each other. It's a learning process' (V).

For these respondents, know-how is better transmitted through daily exchanges, especially through imitation, than through general instructions sent from far away.

Drawing upon the Partners' Complementarities

Cooperation experience makes learning about local cultures and finding appropriate adjustments to work with partners possible. Adjustment does not mean behaving in Rome like the Romans. Adjustments may consist in making the most of differences and mobilizing complementary assets, for instance, the Vietnamese partners provide their knowledge of the local context, which allows for the evaluation of what may be realistically done, or not. 'The Vietnamese team tries to come up with realistic ideas so that the project manager can better manage the project' (V).

The Vietnamese are also the only ones to have access to the local social networks that are essential to get enough support for successful projects. Without prior relationships and insertion in the social network, the French would not obtain the expected involvement of Vietnamese partners. A project exclusively supported by foreigners from outside the social system would have few chances of success. 'If you work only among foreigners, there will not be any good results. Because, even if you have a good methodology and you are well trained, you cannot understand the Vietnamese system of relationships' (V).

Conversely, when dealing with authorities, the young Vietnamese do not feel free to speak up to defend their views. Foreigners may have advantages there; in some cases, they may benefit from a kind of prestige related to accomplishments they have had abroad. Furthermore, as they keep outside of the local social networks, they are not submitted to the informal yet powerful obligations that apply to the members of the networks.

> It's good to work with foreigners. We can go straight to the point. If we are only among Vietnamese, I think it's a bit difficult. If we work with foreigners, it's easier in the relations with the local authorities. With foreigners, they accept propositions more easily because they think that foreign specialists have more experience and know the issues better than the Vietnamese people. With a local partner, it's easier if we say: 'the French have decided …'(V)

As the French are outside the system, they are less sensitive to the power games played by Vietnamese institutions. A Vietnamese interviewee explains: 'If things take place when a foreigner is present, that's good, it's more objective if foreigners talk. When there are only Vietnamese people, it's too subjective' (V).

This strategy called 'one foot in, one foot out' and formalized in a document of the non-governmental organization (Lamballe et al., 2002), seems effective to French managers too:

> We had really found a balance. She knew how to involve me to defend our project when needed and reciprocally, I used her regularly to make things move forwards. We were complementary for operations and for institutional matters. There are a lot of meetings where foreigners are never invited, and decision is made among Vietnamese. Having a counterpart with whom we get along very well to make things move forward is very important ... She may phone to the teams directly in Vietnamese to get some information I could not get. (F)

The French attendance in meetings brings rigour in control but without the Vietnamese contributions, the French would never have access to information to exert this reinforced control.

As time passes, mutual or unilateral learning takes place but, most often, it depends upon clear-sighted individuals who are able to draw empirically upon their experience. However, most aspects of the cultural sense-making systems remain hidden to them. The cooperation could be improved by developing a more formalized approach to foster cross-cultural understanding and to set up a frame for collective action that bridges the gap between the French and Vietnamese sense-making systems.

RECOMMENDATIONS: BUILDING UP A SHARED FRAME FOR COLLECTIVE ACTION

A two-step approach is suggested to improve cross-cultural cooperation. The first step consists in improving mutual perceptions through making explicit the respective cultural sense-making system. The second one aims at capitalizing on the knowledge of both cultures to set up a modus vivendi.

Defusing Negative Perceptions by Making Political Cultures Explicit

A better cross-cultural cooperation requires that both sides understand the other's sense-making system. Evidencing the others' cultural interpretations makes it possible to give appropriate meaning to the partners' actions and may reverse negative feelings. For instance, the change of mind by the Vietnamese collaborator compared to what was prepared (in our first example) sounded at best as a lack of coherence and at worst as a betrayal. In light of the Vietnamese sense-making system linking roles and obligations, this appears now as a loyal behaviour towards one's community. Or what was perceived as French arrogance and the refusal to lend a hand now appears as respectful to the partner's professional autonomy.

Discovering another system of meaning may also result in a change of practices. For example, avoiding contradicting hierarchy, as most Vietnamese do, is not immutable. If foreign managers convey another conception of hierarchical relationships, beyond their initial surprise, most Vietnamese adapt pretty quickly. 'Now, it seems normal to me to make criticisms to improve things. Before, I could not stand it' (V).

Creating a Modus Vivendi Beyond Differences

Knowledge about the partner's cultural references does not alone lead to setting up acceptable ways of working together, either because adopting the other's method is perceived as a regression or because the protagonists still cannot think of appropriate ways to reconcile their different views. It is not possible to bring any definite solution to this problem since appropriate ways of working together are necessarily contingent to the actors' specific cultural representations. The following example shows that common practices may be developed in Franco-Vietnamese cooperation because it makes sense in both frames of meanings.

Learning, which is expected in hierarchical relationships, is an important issue, shared and highly valued by most respondents and considered as a crucial part of the cooperation process. The youth of most of the GRET employees increases their desire to learn, but the older managers are also motivated by learning through cooperation.

As learning is highly valued in both contexts, it could become a starting point to define the role of project managers. The image of the guide, explicitly mentioned by a few Vietnamese respondents and the image of the master in the famous traditional guilds (*'compagnonnage'*) in the French context, may converge to make sense of the cooperation relationship. This reference image gives a positive meaning to the objectively unbalanced relationship between the manager and their team worker. They give value to all actors because these unbalanced relationships are by nature temporary since the student is bound to equal or even surpass the master. What kind of interactional behaviour these images imply and what form the learning relationship should take remain to be explored in detail.

CONCLUSION

This case shows how differences in actors' conception of the world may alter the cooperation in Franco–Vietnamese collaboration. If now, the very existence of cultural differences is acknowledged in managerial literature, the right way to carry out common action in cross-cultural contexts is far from being identified. Some experiments are conducted here and there by facilitators who help international teams but theoretical frameworks to ground the elaboration of cross-culturally bound practices are still missing. What is at stake is not only the success of cooperation projects but also the success of all the cross-cultural situations at work, situations that tend to become standard rather than exceptional.

NOTE

1.   (V) denotes a Vietnamese interviewee, (F) denotes a French interviewee.

REFERENCES

Brannen, M.Y. and J.E. Salk (2000), 'Partnering across borders: negotiating organizational culture in a German-Japanese joint-venture', *Human Relations*, **53**(4), 451–87.
d'Iribarne, P. (1989), *La logique de l'honneur*, Paris: Seuil.
d'Iribarne, P. (2009), 'National cultures and organisations in search of a theory', *International Journal of Cross-Cultural Management*, **9**(3), 309–21.
DiStefano, J.J. and M.L. Maznevski (2000), 'Creating value with diverse teams in global management', *Organizational Dynamics*, **29**(1), 49–63.
Lamballe, P., C. Van Sau, P. Lavigne Delville and G. Rosner (2002), *Mobiliser les acteurs dans une démarche de recherche-action; stratégies institutionnelles et mode de gestion d'un programme de développement rural expérimental dans les collines du Nord-Vietnam*, Coopérer aujourd'hui no. 31, Nogent-sur-Marne, France: GRET Groupe de recherche et d'échanges technologiques.

5. The intercultural challenges in the transfer of codes of conduct from the US to Europe

Christoph I. Barmeyer and Eric Davoine

INTRODUCTION

In the process of internationalization, multinational companies (MNCs) are confronted with the challenge of harmonizing corporate culture throughout their subsidiaries, following the widely held idea that a strong global corporate culture will strengthen the company's identity and image and reduce transaction costs within the MNC. Codes of conduct can be defined as instruments to implement a normative 'global organizational culture', proposing orientations for action in order to control and to regulate the employee behaviours and practices in every subsidiary. Previous studies underlined the US-American tradition of codes of conduct and showed a certain resistance in some European countries towards this kind of normative instrument. Nevertheless, more and more European companies have adopted – and adapted – codes of conduct or ethical codes. We use a case study of a US-based MNC to show how complex the intercultural challenges of the implementation of codes of conduct in European subsidiaries are. Our case study in different French and German subsidiaries of the same US company, through in-depth interviews with managers from different professional sub-groups and sub-cultures, shows a very divergent picture of this resistance.

CASE PRESENTATION

Codes of Conduct: An Instrument of North American Origin

Corporate codes of conduct or ethical codes set out a formalization of detailed rules that aim to guide the employee in their decisions and daily behaviour in and outside the company (Gauthier, 2000; Mercier, 2001).

The code of conduct represents a reference frame of values, principles and norms that must be integrated by the employee in the process of organizational socialization. For the MNC, codes of conduct can also be considered as an instrument of control and regulation of subsidiaries or foreign suppliers. In providing this common reference frame to all employees, regardless of the national legal environment of local subsidiaries, the MNC is called on to play a greater institutional role, easily assimilated to 'a legislator' without state (Arthurs, 2006).

Lastly, codes of conduct can be considered as an instrument formalizing a normative 'corporate culture' that aims to define a common identity for the members of the organization, as well as orienting, conditioning or even regulating the actions and decisions of the members of the organization by putting routines, cognitive schemes and values at their disposal. In the MNC, the question of the normative 'corporate culture' is even more complex as it implies the adequacy of values, norms and practices often defined at the level of the parent company together with the different contexts of the subsidiaries, particularly with the contexts of the national cultures (Schneider and Barsoux, 2003).

As an instrument of behaviour regulation through culture, codes of conduct or ethical codes are not 'culturally neutral' instruments: the instrument comes from the US and takes its significance in the history and in the institutional and cultural context of the country. The study of Langlois and Schlegelmilch (1990) clearly shows that at the end of the 1980s, the phenomenon of ethical codes concerned more the North American multinationals than the European multinationals: only 41 per cent of European multinationals in their sample have a code against 75 per cent of the large multinationals of the US. The most recent study of Kaptein (2004) on the 200 largest multinationals gives prominence to similar proportions as he observes that today 68 per cent of the 59 largest North American multinationals have this type of code, against 45 per cent of the largest German or French multinationals and 38 per cent of Japanese ones. These percentages concern only multinationals and probably underestimate the differences between Europe and the US that are probably more important for medium-size companies.

Diffused in the US at the end of the 1970s following the Foreign Corrupt Practices Act (1977), codes of conduct or ethical codes are embedded in the American tradition of 'internal company regulations' specific to the nineteenth century. These internal regulations instituted the obligations of individuals towards a community through a contractual and explicit form that was necessary in the immigrant society of the US (Seidel, 1995). In this American society of the nineteenth century, the company could be assigned an ethical role because individual and moral interests were tightly linked: be it in the community conceptions of Puritanism or in the ones of the individualistic utilitarian, morality was perceived as useful since it was a source of material success (d'Iribarne, 2002). In the US, the company of the nineteenth century had thus a legitimate ethical actor that it seems to have conserved today; the introduction of the Sarbanes-Oxley Act (SOX, 2002) has even strengthened this position.

For authors like d'Iribarne (2002) in France or Palazzo (2002) in Germany, the adoption of ethically formalized instruments as codes of conduct is bound to encounter difficulties and resistance in some European countries, because their cultural conceptions of ethics are different from North American conceptions. Codes of conduct can be defined as tools or organizational practices that are strongly 'value infused' (Blazejewski, 2006) and marked by an Anglo-Saxon universalistic perception of rules, an explicit and formalized communication style and the implicit agreement that companies can be legitimate setters of ethical rules (Palazzo, 2002).

Analysing the Reception of Codes in French and German Subsidiaries of AMIE

In order to analyse these transfer processes, we carried out a study on the reception of the 2003 version of the code of conduct in the French and German subsidiaries of the US multinational corporation AMIE. The objective was to compare the reception of US 'value infused' instruments in two different European national environments that are very different from a cultural or institutional perspective (Barmeyer and Davoine, 2006).

AMIE is a company in the chemicals sector with more than 40 000 employees worldwide. The German and French subsidiaries, respectively, have about 1000 and 2500 employees and were founded in the 1960s. The headquarters of AMIE in the US is in the Midwest. In Germany, the group had three units: a production site in the North of Germany resulting from the fusion with a German site from another group (about 300 employees), the German headquarters (with commercial and research and development (R&D) activities) and a centre for packaging and logistics in the region of Frankfurt. In France, the group had two locations: a production site in the East of France (1500 employees) and the French headquarters along with the marketing and sales departments in the region of Paris. Since the beginning of the twentieth century, AMIE has developed a discourse centred on three fundamental values for its employees that has developed progressively into a code of conduct through the twentieth century.

The 2003 version of the code comprises 30 pages that precisely describe norms of professional behaviour articulated around the three values. The code of conduct is conceived by the headquarters and presents behaviours to follow in different problematical situations (conflicts of interest, corruption, confidential information, respect of the environment, respect of others, health and security and so on). Employees in every subsidiary are supposed to sign the last page of the code at the same time as their work contract. This signature represents a moral commitment of the employee with respect to their employer. In case of observed violations of the code, employees are supposed to inform the headquarters by using a hotline with a toll-free number. The codes of conduct are written and translated at the American headquarters and the human resources (HR) departments of the subsidiaries only have a right to see the quality of the translation. In addition to the code, each employee of the company is given another guideline of 'Good Management Practices' that specifically corresponds to their work field (sales, buying, R&D and so on) and which they must also take into consideration.

To analyse the reception of the code, we carried out a documentary study on the HR instruments used within the group and conducted a series of interviews with 21 managers and employee representatives of the German and French subsidiaries. We used different types of conceptual frames and collections of data to diversify the perspectives of interpretation and assure a 'triangulation' of the data (Yin, 1990). Half of the managers met were HR managers responsible for the implementation of the code of conduct. Half of the interlocutors met had an expatriation experience in the American parent company. Each interview lasted between 60 and 90 minutes and was structured following the same guidelines. Two German HR managers and two French HR managers were seen many times during the documentary study and before and after the series of interviews. Thus, about ten additional hours of interview were conducted in each country. Finally, a presentation of the results to the managers gave an internal validation to our conclusions. Given the international and intercultural context of the interactions in the field, the interviews in both countries were conducted in the mother tongue of the interviewee. The interviews were conducted and analysed by two researchers, one French researcher and one German, to minimize cultural biases, or even ethnocentric biases, of the observations (Marschan-Piekkari et al., 2004).

CASE ANALYSIS

Critics Addressed to the Code's Content and Formulation

The first type of critics addressed to the code concerns its content and its formulations: the code is strongly inspired by the North American legal frame and comprises a number of references to American laws. These references do not provoke open resistances within the local subsidiaries, but they indicate too explicitly the 'country of origin' of the instrument. This gives it an ethnocentric characteristic that makes it lose credibility and legitimacy with the European subsidiaries' personnel. 'For example, some things are very US, "you must contact the lawyer", the reference to the US boycott law, this makes you smile because culturally speaking we are not in the same context, here, we do not call a lawyer for a single case' (French, Quality manager). 'The illustrations are very American, for example, the women, the minorities and the "colored people", and the style remains very naive. It makes everyone here laugh, notably the naivety of the example on sexual harassment' (French, Management controller).

For the French managers interviewed, the strong confinement of the North American culture within the code of conduct is viewed as exotic or even as inadaptable: 'For Americans, especially in the Midwest, they can exhibit [the code] in their bedroom. It is a very conservative culture, it fits them like a glove. It doesn't occur to them that it could be done otherwise' (French, Quality manager). The Midwestern approach poses a problem, especially to the French, who demand the freedom of interpretation in the respect of rules: 'We accept it, we sign, but the position is rather "OK, if at times I go over the top, it's manageable"' (French, Quality manager).

Our observations confirm Philippe d'Iribarne's (2002) thesis of a French cultural resistance to the moralistic dimension (the notion of catechism is regularly mentioned) of the codes of conduct: 'It is a little bit like what we learn in catechism. (… here in France) we can take some freedom with it' (French, HR manager). In the same manner, many testimonials insist on the notion of free will in the interpretation of the rule in which French employees and managers rely in particular circumstances:

> France is another planet. There is such aggressiveness and permanent infringement of regulations, just watch simply the traffic on the roads … During the meeting on 'compliance' with the management members [French], we received a call from the police which interrupted the meeting because ten cars were not parked properly outside. Sixty managers of all levels who speak of compliance and who are not parked properly … (French, Operations manager)

In the German subsidiaries, critics have been conveyed to the code but in a more moderate manner than in French subsidiaries. A recurring reproach made to the parent company is not having allowed the participation of the local actors to its elaboration, which would be more in the spirit of the local institutional context.

> The first version was not very easy to understand. There were so many mistakes and problems with the translation, and some contradictions with German labor law too. We reformulated some points, not necessarily because of the content but mostly because of the style, and send it back to the headquarters. But they did not want to see our point of view first. (German, HR manager)

> Examples are very American and there is often a lack of credibility. For instance: 'you should not speak about your company at a private party'. Do you think that I

go to parties to speak with my friends about business? (German, Marketing manager)

The German managers met sometimes blamed the directness of the code ('I find that the code is often commanding in its manner to teach us things'), its moralistic intrusions in the private sphere ('As if we would go to a party just to divulge all the company secrets!'), rarely its North American identity: 'In the beginning, I found the red book to be very American. I found that it was a little exaggerated. The values gave me the same effect as the promotional messages of Nike or Coke. But it was just my first impression' (German, Administrative manager).

The individuals professionally socialized within a German subsidiary of an American group (be it in AMIE or in another), and managers with an expatriate experience in the US were less surprised than the others, as they were familiar with this type of practice, which is common in North American groups.

The Conflicts Between the Code and the Legal Frame

It is the dimension of internal regulation in the content that poses the most important problem because German and French labor laws foresee a specific procedure for the admission of an internal regulation that involves the participation of local personnel representatives. The French social law (disposal of Article L. 122–36 in the code of labour) foresees the consultation of representatives of the personnel, with a validation of the *Comité d'établissement* (French work council) on a '*règlement interne*'. The fact of going beyond this procedure makes this code an instrument of regulation without legal value. In the same manner, the German legal frame (Betriebsverfassungsgesetz, 2006) foresees that an internal set of rules must be accepted officially by the representatives of the *Betriebsrat* (German work council). Yet, such acceptance procedures would probably lead to demands of modification that are incompatible with the will of the parent company to implement the same unique code in all the subsidiaries.

In France as well as in Germany, the clause 'The collaborators breaking the law, the Code or the Good Management Practices, risk disciplinary measures that can lead to their discharge' leads to assimilate the code as an internal regulation that can serve as a basis for legal sanction. The 'Novartis jurisprudence' (family court of Nanterre, 6 October 2004) has since annulled the lay-off of an employee from the French subsidiary of the Swiss group Novartis, justified by an offence to the corporate code of conduct, by invoking the fact that the code could not act as an internal regulation because it did not respect legal procedure. This single clause of disciplinary measure in the event of an offence thus renders every reference to the code as legally risky at the moment of sanctions and even of a negative assessment of the personnel. The code loses all form of legitimacy and its functionality of regulation: 'We are currently asked not to use it as a reference when speaking of behaviour. But it is legally impossible to fire a collaborator by making a reference to the code because it is not an internal regulation ... it is putting the entire code in question' (French, HR manager).

The legal department of AMIE France asked that the page referring to the possible measures of sanctions should be modified. The US headquarters refused any local adaptation of the content that would make the document lose the essence of the unique standard applicable to all subsidiaries. Unable to modify the text of the code, the HR departments of the French and German companies chose not to follow the validation procedure of the internal regulation. Instead of this, they gave their employees the code accompanied by a letter from the president of the national subsidiaries stating that the code would be applied within the boundaries of the actual legal frame of the country. In the letter, the request to commit to the content was replaced by the request to confirm being informed of the content. This measure has enabled a high rate (around 97 percent in France like in Germany, according to HR departments), but not absolute, of returned signatures from employees having 'been informed' of the new version of the code. It is actually a pyrrhic victory: the US headquarters won and imposed an unchanged text, but the code has lost its meaning and finality as a regulation and standardization instrument.

Differentiated Local Resistances

The legal frame has been used as an instrument of resistance by the actors of the subsidiaries, but not in a systematic manner within the different French and German sites. In France, only the representatives of the personnel from the Paris site, affiliated to a trade union, have asked that the code be put on the agenda in the committee meetings, following instruction from the national trade union after the Novartis jurisprudence. The representatives of the personnel from the production site in the East of France, without trade union representatives, did not react to the notice regarding the new version of the code: The work council members of the French production site, even if they often blamed the content of the code for being 'too American', did not oppose its diffusion. Considering the historically good industrial relations of the site, they felt the code could even serve as a support to restructure a corporate culture that was threatened to weaken with the recent expansion of the site.

In Germany, personnel representatives of the site in Frankfurt posed no problems and no demands. On the site in Frankfurt, the relations between employer and the employee representatives have been historically good and the codes of conduct have existed since the beginning of the company.

However, personnel representatives of the site in Northern Germany reacted very critically to the code and encouraged the personnel of the northern German site not to sign the letters from management. The northern German site is marked by a more conflictual history linked to a merger with the dominating role of AMIE. The employees have been socialized before the merger on a site with a former strong German identity, where the German institutional framework of co-determination (Betriebsverfassungsgesetz, 2006) played an important role. The personnel representatives and employees of the site could feel their traditional rights threatened by a code of conduct that represents an instrument coming from another national context and from a parent company perceived as dominant. The historic relation between headquarter-subsidiary of the sites played an important role to explain the different reactions towards the code.

IMPLICATIONS FOR CROSS-CULTURAL MANAGEMENT

Our case study in the French and German subsidiaries of a US MNC shows that the implementation of codes of conduct is a difficult task when the code is implemented without adaptation and without consideration to the local cultural and institutional environment (Kostova and Roth, 2002; Tempel et al., 2006). Codes of conduct are intended to create international coherence and cultural standardization, but the generally hesitant and problematic reception process indicates that precisely the will of homogenization is the cause of disagreement. On the basis of our findings we can stress some implications for cross-cultural management.

The case study shows that a code of conduct or ethical codes, as HR-instrument of behaviour regulation through culture, is not 'culturally neutral': the instrument comes from the US and makes sense in a specific institutional and cultural context. Our study confirms the former conclusions of d'Iribarne (2002) and Palazzo (2002) that codes can provoke critical reactions or resistance in a French or in a German context. Most of the employees of the French and German subsidiaries of AMIE do not react positively to the code, to its moralistic formulations, to some specific parts of the content (control of private life, whistleblowing and so on) and to some principles and values the code is based on, for example, the universalistic respect of rules (Trompenaars, 1993) and of standards set by an employer without discussion with the local workforce representatives. Many of them seemed to find the code meaningless because it did not fit with their values and their beliefs. At the same time, we observed that French and German managers with an expatriate experience within the headquarters were able to understand and to explain the US cultural and institutional context in which the codes have been developed – and the problems encountered during the transfer in a new context. During the transfer process, these managers played an important role in explaining the intended meaning of the code to the French or to the German staff.

The case study has also emphasized that a code of conduct cannot be introduced with the same legal value in European subsidiaries. Codes of conduct are normative instruments of extremely fragile legitimacy when not adapted to the local frameworks of industrial relations. At the same time, the differentiated analysis of the local actor strategies also shows that resistance is not a cultural or institutional automatism: not all the subsidiary actors use the possibilities of the institutional context to resist the headquarters. The differences observed on the sites clearly show that the organizational context, the history and the identity of each site, as well as the individual strategies of local actors play an important role in the phenomenon of resistance. Our case confirms the need, in the analysis of the cross-cultural transfer of management instruments or organizational practices, of a differentiated approach that would take into consideration different levels of analysis (see, for instance, Geppert et al., 2003; Kostova, 1999): cultural proximity of the instrument 'infused values' with the local contexts, institutional adaptability of the instrument, organizational context and relationship between the parent company and the subsidiary, individual and collective strategies of local actors.

RECOMMENDATIONS TO PRACTITIONERS

Codes of conduct, as an instrument that aims to regulate actions and decisions in subsidiaries, are instruments that are particularly difficult to be transferred in a standardized way. Managers should learn from the case that it is probably impossible to standardize a MNC corporate culture with the help of an instrument that is so profoundly embedded in the specific national legal frame and rooted in the cultural history of the parent company. Finding ways to adapt the instrument to local legal and cultural constraints is the first recommendation we can formulate to practitioners. Especially in the German context, we could identify a clear will of contributing to the code, discussing and adapting the code to local requirements and contingencies in order to develop a legitimated and adapted instrument. That would make the code lose its character of a unique and homogeneous set of standards throughout the MNC, but it would make it more useful to control the local subsidiaries. In the current situation, without adaptation, the 'implemented' code has no legal value, neither in France nor in Germany, and can simply not be used legally as a reference frame of rules and standards.

A discussion on the local adaptation and on the local interpretation of the code can be worthwhile for the relationship between parent company and subsidiary because it will reveal differences of perceptions, values and expectations, and let the actors make explicit their meanings of corporate values and orientations, and their meanings of conducts and (business) practices. It is not enough to present and train the elements of corporate culture as a 'simple' directive from the parent company. Rather, participants taking part in such a training measure should first be familiarized with the fundamental assumptions of the national culture of the parent company. These should then be related to the fundamental assumptions of the national culture of the subsidiary. Then the national cultural values as well as the corporate cultural values can be put into perspective. Such a discussion would bring the actors to share meanings of business conducts and situations, and would therefore impact more the constitution of the corporate culture than the signature of a locally meaningless document.

Managers with experience of both cultural environments of the parent company and of the subsidiary could play a major role in the discussion about adapting management instruments and organizational practices by explaining the meaning of the instruments and practices in the national context of the parent company. They could act as 'cultural translators' and help the MNC to minimize conflicts and misunderstandings that result from different ways of thinking, communicating and working within the subsidiaries. It is useful to have managers with an experience of the US headquarters in France and in Germany, but it would certainly be useful as well to have European expatriates or impatriates within the headquarters and discussing the relevance of ethnocentric instruments in the different regions of the world. In the end, international human resources development, especially professional training and expatriation policy, plays a crucial role in the transfer of management tools and organizational practices, especially when the practices are so strongly 'value infused' like codes of conduct.

REFERENCES

Arthurs, H.W. (2006), 'Corporate codes of conduct: profit, power and law in the global economy', in W. Cragg (ed.), *Ethics Codes, Corporation and the Challenge of Globalization*, Cheltenham, UK and Northampton, MA, USA: Edward Elgar, pp. 51–74.

Barmeyer, C.I. and E. Davoine, (2006) 'International corporate cultures: from helpless global convergence to constructive European divergence', in C. Scholz and J. Zentes (eds), *Strategic Management – New Rules for Old Europe?*, Wiesbaden: Gabler, pp. 227–45.

Betriebsverfassungsgesetz (BetrVG) (2006), 'Mitwirkung und Mitbestimmung der Arbeitnehmer', Absätze 74–113, in *Arbeitsgesetze*, Munich: DTV, pp. 591–610.

Blazejewski, S. (2006), 'Transferring value infused organizational practices in multinational companies', in M. Geppert and M. Mayer (eds), *Global, National and Local Practices in Multinational Companies*, Houndmills: Palgrave Macmillan, pp. 63–104.

d'Iribarne, P. (2002), 'La légitimité de l'entreprise comme acteur éthique aux Etats-Unis et en France', *Revue Française de Gestion*, **28**(140), 23–39.

Gauthier, L. (2000), 'L'impact des chartes d'éthique', *Revue Française de Gestion*, **130**, 77–88.

Geppert, M., K. Williams and D. Matten (2003), 'The social construction of contextual rationalities in MNCs: an Anglo-German comparison of subsidiary choice', *Journal of Management Studies*, **40**(3), 617–41.

Kaptein, M. (2004), 'Business codes of multinational firms: what do they say?', *Journal of Business Ethics*, **50**(1), 13–31.

Kostova, T. (1999), 'Transnational transfer of strategic organizational practices. A contextual perspective', *Academy of Management Review*, **24**(2), 308–24.

Kostova, T. and K. Roth (2002), 'Adoption of an organizational practice by subsidiaries of multinational corporations: institutional and relational effects', *Academy of Management Journal*, **45**(1), 215–33.

Langlois, C.C. and B.B. Schlegelmilch (1990), 'Do corporate codes of ethics reflect national character? Evidence from Europe and the US', *Journal of International Business Studies,* **21**(4), 519–39.

Marschan-Piekkari, R., C. Welch, H. Penttinen and M. Tahvanainen (2004), 'Interviewing in the multinational corporation: challenges of the organizational context', in R. Marschan-Piekkari and C. Welch (eds), *Handbook of Qualitative Research Methods for International Business*, Cheltenham, UK and Northampton, MA, USA: Edward Elgar, pp. 244–63.

Mercier, S. (2001), 'Institutionnaliser l'éthique dans les grandes entreprises françaises', *Revue Française de Gestion*, **136**, 62–9.

Palazzo, B. (2002), 'U.S.-American and German business ethics: an intercultural comparison', *Journal of Business Ethics*, **41**(3), 195–216.

Schneider, S.C. and J.-L. Barsoux (2003), *Managing Across Cultures*, 2nd edn, Essex: Pearson.

Seidel, F. (ed.) (1995), *L'Ethique des affaires et de l'entreprise*, Paris: Editions ESKA.

Sarbanes-Oxley Act (2002), Section 406 of the Sarbanes-Oxley Act of 2002; SEC Item 406 of Regulation S-K; NASDAQ Rule 4350(n) and NYSE Listed Company Manual Section 303A(10) http://www.soxlaw.com.

Tempel, A., H. Waechter and P. Walenbach (2006), 'The comparative institutional approach to HRM in multinational companies', in M. Geppert and M. Mayer (eds), *Global, National and Local Practices in Multinational Companies*, Houndmills: Palgrave Macmillan, pp. 17–37.

Trompenaars, F. (1993), *Riding the Waves of Culture. Understanding Cultural Diversity in Business*, London: The Economists Books

Yin, R.K. (1990), *Case Study Research: Design and Methods,* 2nd edn, Thousand Oaks, CA: Sage.

6. When American management system meets Tunisian culture: the Poulina case

Hèla Yousfi[1]

INTRODUCTION

Can companies in developing countries modernize despite their local cultural context, by struggling against it or by simply importing so-called 'universal' standards developed in the West? Or can such companies leverage valuable aspects of each local culture and use them to modernize management practices?

Scholars who focus on management in developing countries generally fall into two camps: 'Organizational Theorists' and 'Culturalists'. The former hold that the theoretical principles underlying organizational behaviour are universal in all countries. The latter argue that management practices in developing countries are rooted in local cultural values. However, when it comes to recommendations for modernizing firms in developing countries, the gap between the two camps is not as large as it first appears; both advocate a best practice – or 'one best way' – approach (Leonard, 1987).

Several examples show that simply adopting 'best management practices' will not improve developing countries' economic performance (Yousfi, 2007a). Some management tools that experts propose do not have the desired effects, and companies often abandon them after the experts leave. Furthermore, while some companies do achieve substantial technical and financial success (AFD, 1998), most reformers promoting developing countries' integration into the global economy ascribe the results solely to 'universal' methods: few will examine the concrete aspects of these singular successes and their effective achievements. This makes it impossible to distinguish what is genuinely universal in so-called 'universal' management methods from elements that reflect the unique features of their originating context (d'Iribarne et al., 2007; Yousfi, 2010).

This chapter draws upon a Tunisian company, Poulina, which has implemented American management techniques, and questions the appropriateness of imposing a unique management model on companies in developing countries.[1] I will first briefly present the case and then show the relevance of d'Iribarne's conceptualization of culture (1989, 2009) for challenges to management modernization in developing countries: a summary of empirical findings will follow. Finally, I will discuss how the Poulina case challenges earlier assumptions about the role of culture in transferring management techniques, as well as its implications for practitioners. Two factors are crucial to my conclusions. First, the imported tools should meet locally defined expectations of 'good management'. Second, these tools' adoption depends heavily on their reinterpretation according to local cultural references.

CASE PRESENTATION

Culture and Management in Tunisia

Tunisia is the northernmost country in Africa: bordering the Mediterranean, it occupies a strategic position with direct links to Europe, North and West Africa and the Middle East. Tunisia has developed its tourism, agricultural, manufacturing and mining sectors, gaining a leading position as an emerging market in Africa. For the last 20 years, Tunisia has concentrated on privatization and integration into the global economy, making it attractive for foreign investment.

Tunisian culture arises from more than three thousand years of history and reflects a mix of significant religious and ethnic influences, including Christians and Muslims and the Carthaginians, Romans, Arabs, Turks, French and native Berbers. Tunisia has many cultural particularities: it is crucial to understand them in order to implement effective management practices.

Tunisian managers use an entrepreneurial, family-based model as a reference point. As R. Zghal (1989) has shown, this affects Tunisian companies in two ways. First, organizations are conceived as systems of relationships, where personal networks and social positioning are important. The organization achieves its goals by deploying and managing these relationships. Feelings take precedence over formal task definitions, creating a reluctance to establish strict formal rules for dealing with certain problems. Where rules must be established, they are deliberately vague and subject to diverse interpretations, with individual responsibilities loosely or poorly defined. Second, there is strong attachment to two values: equality – rooted in Islamic culture – and dignity associated with the Mediterranean code of honour, giving paternalistic relationships a very specific role. Paternalism is a form of supervision that allows the worker to overcome symbolically the otherwise humiliating subordinate role. It also allows for a charismatic style of leadership, one preferred in cases where authority must be exerted. This organizational system can be very effective in a context of good relationships, but can prove equally problematic when the leader's authority comes into question.

Poulina: A Successful Company

Poulina is one of the largest private companies in North Africa, ranking among the 40 leading African companies according to the Boston Consulting Group (June 2010). It reflects the successful transformation of a small, ten-employee company worth $20 000 to a group of 70 companies worth $700 million and employing 15 000 people. Since its creation in 1967 by a few visionary businessmen led by Abdel Waheb Ben Ayed, the Poulina Group's activities have ranged from agriculture to construction and tourism inside Tunisia and abroad in Libya, Algeria, France, Martinique and elsewhere. The Group's outstanding performance is marked by great complementarities between various interconnected divisions and a high return on investment. The implementation of modern management tools – often qualified as 'American' by the employees interviewed – are widely perceived as central to Poulina's success story. In fact, this successful company differs most strikingly from other Tunisian companies in its use of strict rules and an employee performance appraisal system directly inspired by the American management model.

Data Collection

To understand the dynamics behind Poulina's successful implementation of the American management system, I used an ethnographic approach (d'Iribarne, 1989; Geertz, 1973), conducting field interviews to understand how imported management techniques fit with Tunisian employees' conceptions of what constitutes 'good management'. I conducted approximately 40 interviews in May and June 2004 with management and workers at various levels within the head office and two subsidiaries. I recorded the interviews and then translated them literally. All quotations below are respondents' comments. I deliberately give a very broad place to the interviewees' discourse, to allow readers to form their own picture of Poulina's management beyond the analysis I propose. This approach allows an analysis of how the respondents interpreted the new tools and then implemented them.

Culture is seen specifically as providing 'frames of meaning' for each society – frameworks that shape concepts about the way people should be governed. In other words, culture is not referred to in terms of customs and values nor shared identities (Hofstede, 1980), but rather for the implicit representations underlying the practices and discourses of people with regard to organization and cooperation (d'Iribarne, 2009; d'Iribarne et al., 1998). The merit of this approach lies in its capacity to clarify conditions that make up 'good' management within a Tunisian context, and show the way culture affects the transfer of imported management tools into Tunisian companies.

Thus, the analysis focused on how interviewees used language to construct and convey meanings for Poulina's new, imported management tools. It included identifying the metaphors interviewees used to suggest what constitutes good management or what good cooperation is or should be like. The analysis also tracked the words, expressions, repetitions and emphasis used to formulate comments and opinions about the various changes introduced by the American management tools.

CASE ANALYSIS

Our respondents stress the introduction of American management techniques as a key factor in Poulina's success. Yet, on closer examination, the interviews show that the success of the 'American' tools depended on their 'Tunisian' reinterpretation, that is, making them meaningful for their users. First, I shall outline how the interviewees described the transfer of American management techniques. Second, I shall analyse the Tunisian employees' reinterpretation of them and show how culture influences implementation of imported management tools. The crucial dynamic behind the successful transfer at Poulina will thus emerge: coherence between core aspects of the new management tools and local expectations of what 'good management' should be. This dynamic, combined with the reinterpretative process, helps make sense of these tools according to local frames of meanings. It is worth noting that in addition to reinterpreting them during initial implementation, Poulina's managers and workers have adjusted and adapted the imported tools over the years. Interestingly, rather than contrasting with local cultural practices, these adaptations build on them (see Yousfi et al., 2005). In this chapter, I deliberately chose to focus only on the employees' process of making sense of the transferred tools.

Introducing 'American Management System'

In American companies, working relations rest on contracts that determine what is regulated and to what degree, whether in relations between a superior and his subordinate, relations between supplier and client, or, in unionized companies, relations between the corporation and the union (Foner, 1998). Contracts rest on notions of fair exchange and equity, such that both parties retain their rights, preserving autonomy and self-determination. Individuals receive rewards according to their individual contribution and if it is not recognized, they are prepared to move on. This 'contractual' view of an organization has an achievement orientation, focusing on goals and meeting objectives. Bosses and subordinates are expected to engage in a two-way dialogue to agree on what has to be done, by when and how. Many human resources practices, such as performance appraisals, equal opportunity recruitment and promotions, are heavily embedded in this contractual view of organizations, and are designed to avoid lawsuits.

Using an ethnographic approach, Philippe d'Iribarne (1989, 2009) showed that the American organizational model – a reference point throughout the world – is rooted in a specifically American culture, and reflects a political ideal of a society based on contracts freely entered into by equals (Tocqueville, 1835). This contractual ideal parallels a great mistrust of the arbitrariness of power, and a great faith in recourse to objectivity as a means of avoiding this arbitrariness (Locke, 1980). The question thus becomes: how do we explain the successful implementation of the American management model in Poulina given the differences between the model's inherent cultural assumptions and the Tunisian cultural context?

What American Management System was Introduced in Poulina?

Interview respondents evoked values such as 'transparency', 'accountability', 'rigour' and 'meritocracy' to explain Poulina's success. Top management explained that the American model largely inspired the quest to implement such values: 'We are adopting the American management system that allows each employee to be responsible for his work and to see his objectives … People are judged on the basis of their achievements. If they cannot fulfil their objectives, they are held responsible.'

Respondents emphasized that this contractual logic was Poulina's chief borrowing from the American management model. Each employee who joins Poulina has a contract based on four elements: a job description the employee discusses with their boss, work objectives, a reporting system, and remuneration based on the reporting system and the objectives achieved.

At first glance, one could easily conclude that if Poulina Group succeeded in setting up an effective management system, it was because they had broken with the traditional Tunisian operations by applying American management formulae. This would confirm the assumption that the only condition required to modernize management in developing countries is to trade off local methods against the so-called 'best practices' that are considered 'universal wisdom'. However, this assumption comes into question if one looks at the respondents' comments, which describe how they actually managed to introduce the new tools and how they motivated people to accept the new system. It is worth noting that top managers used English and/or French during the interviews when they described Poulina's management system, reflecting their training in France or in the US. They switched automatically to their native Tunisian dialect when asked to comment on implementing 'American' management tools, using their own language to describe their own experience in concrete terms.

When the American Management System Meets Local Expectations

Interviews examining Poulina's management practices revealed that if employees favoured implementing American techniques, it was because these tools echoed local expectations for more 'rigour' and emphasized the importance of highly explicit operating procedures. Respondents viewed Poulina's explicitness and formalized policies as means to mitigate the 'dysfunctions' or problems of a family-based model.

Interviewees spoke of these procedures as 'solutions' to identified 'dysfunctions'. A factory operator highlighted the issue: 'Poulina's strong point is to have neutralized the dysfunctions of a family-based model as it prevails in Tunisian companies.' 'Dysfunction' refers here to the interference of personal relationships with work, leading to a great deal of confusion and ambiguity in managing work relationships. As mentioned above, workers' productivity could be affected by the influence – real or imagined – of personal relationships on their career. Moreover, they will judge the boss not on his competence, but on his friendliness and courtesy. His authority may be undermined if he does not come from the same social group as his subordinates. Thus, employees welcomed the explicit, formalized and standardized processes accompanying the American management model because they perceived these as deflecting managers' temptations towards favouritism or corruption.

As one manager pointed out: 'The most important asset of Poulina is the rigor in management secured by well defined procedures ... We make the rules, we follow the rules and we take measures against the person who does not respect the rules.'

When the Management System Borrows Cultural Metaphors

In this section, I shall show Poulina's enduring concern for the delicate balance between a rigorous respect of procedures and the expression of personal bonds. I shall analyse cultural metaphors that recurred in the interviews and helped give meaning to the imported 'American' tools. I argue that Poulina's employees make sense of new management tools via their local Tunisian culture, rather than through the meanings usually associated with these management practices in the US or in a 'new negotiated' culture.

Poulina: A Big Family with Written Rules

Most Tunisian companies are family-owned, which makes it hard to establish a separation between familial and professional relationships. Poulina opted to ban recruitment of 'close relatives' of shareholders to manage the risk of family co-optation behaviour, relying instead on competence as a benchmark. Similarly, our interviewees pointed out that Poulina did manage to get rid of 'the paternal-ist management model' prevalent elsewhere, where the boss is the sole decision maker in the company. In this regard, the introduction of 'American' manage-ment tools – considered 'modern' and 'objective' by our interviewees – appears to mitigate confusing or arbitrary situations that would prevail in other Tunisian companies. Yet, although Poulina's system differs greatly from the family-based model, the family metaphor recurs often in our respondents' accounts as they describe the relationships between superiors and subordinates or between Poulina's head office and its subsidiaries: 'Poulina is an organic group that could be compared to a big family with written rules', explains a director of a subsidiary company. 'Poulina is our mother', comments another employee.

In these responses, one repeatedly finds the positive image of the head office as 'caring father', one who helps his companies and supports them when they achieve good performances. One coordinator explains: 'The role of the head office is to push the subsidiary companies to do their best, to advise them, but the last word is their word: if they achieve a good performance, we tell them "*Sahiit*" [well done], if not we will ask them to be "careful".'

The head office was also described in a more negative, but legitimate, way as an 'authoritarian' father. As one manager put it:

> If we notice one of our companies deviating from plan, we put verbal pressure on the director for one year, then we would put the director under supervision, like a child is under supervision: he will only 'sign papers' (just execute tasks) until he adjusts his behaviour, and if not, he will step down.

The metaphor's value here lies in its capacity for easing and smoothing submission to 'impersonal' and 'cold' rules. In this connection, one of the executives implementing the new performance appraisal procedures explained that he prefers to call the procedures manual a 'user's guide', so employees do not see it as a 'constraint' but rather an aid to improving their performance. In the US performance assessments ultimately focus on achieving specific results, but at Poulina, performance appraisal procedures take on meaning within Tunisian frames of reference. The stress on 'education' and the family metaphor helps employees to cope with the formal constraints of Poulina's management system. At the same time, the rational and formal aspects of the system act as an anonymous antidote to the problems that personal relation-ships could generate.

A Craftsman is Happier than a Worker

Some of our respondents pointed out the large turnover in Poulina's middle management; while this seems principally due to work pressures, another reason is that other Tunisian companies offer wages three times higher than Poulina's to attract the most brilliant candidates. Those who choose Poulina in spite of external temptations stressed their 'autonomy' as a key reason to stay. By using the metaphor of the craftsman, employees underscore that they adhere to strict rules, but in independent ways. Despite their subordinate position, they preserve their 'dignity' and independence through the strategies they adopt in response to such rules. An executive explained this balance as follows:

> To work for others is considered degrading in Tunisia [slavery is the metaphor most often used to describe a subordinate's situation]. As soon as someone starts to succeed in his work, his circle of family and friends pushes him to work for himself. The term 'zoufri', from the French word 'ouvrier' [worker] means 'thug' in Tunisian dialect ... That's why I think the craftsman is happier than a worker. The procedures help people preserve their honour: they are working autonomously, like craftsmen; they are engaged, responsible, they do not have a 'boss' who controls them and who dictates to them what they have to do. At the same time, they can lose their 'honour' if they do not achieve their written objectives

Poulina's chairman (Abdelwaheb Ben Ayed) further amplifies the theme:

> We are inspired by the model of a craftsman working for himself. SNA (a Poulina subsidiary) had sixty-two employees; today they have fifty. The other employees became associates or subcontractors. The craftsman is happier than the worker because he has the feeling he is working for himself and not for an anonymous shareholder. For instance, we give our drivers ownership of their vehicles so they can feel free, and then they do a better job for us. They repay the debt on the vehicle whenever they can. Thus, they manage the vehicles as good fathers and they do their best to deserve our trust ... The same things applies to our shops under the Poulina brand; we give ownership of the shop to the manager ... and so forth.

It is the ideal of a craftsman's autonomy – more than a simple reincarnation of an old artisan model – that gives meaning to the system of relationships between subsidiaries and the head office, or between the superiors and subordinates. This model expresses the autonomy needed to escape 'servile' submission to a boss or to an anonymous ruler. This entrepreneurial dynamic, translated into the metaphor of the 'happy craftsman', transformed Poulina into a place of initiative-taking for small, private production. Poulina offers its employees autonomy to develop their capacities and even to set up their own businesses while also guaranteeing trustworthy relationships with executives who become subcontractors.

A System that Preserves 'Honour'

Respondents often referred to Poulina's management system as a system that preserves 'the honour' of people who adhere to it: 'One feels one is responsible – one does not act in the shadow of somebody else', as an operational manager explained. Moreover, the system's formality allows equal treatment for everyone: 'Everyone is subject to the same rules.' Consequently, employees preserve their 'honour' and are still shielded from their boss's arbitrary use of power. At the same time, they cannot do whatever they want because procedures define what they can and cannot do. As Abdelwaheb Ben Ayed explains:

> Procedures help people preserve their honour. On one hand, they are committed, responsible; they do not have a boss looking over their shoulder who dictates what they must do. On the other hand, they can lose 'face' if they do not achieve written objectives ... If somebody says 'No, I do not agree with something,' we tell him 'OK, go ahead, suggest something.' If he doesn't succeed in proving he is right, he will end up submitting himself to the rule ... The procedures make the relationship between superiors and their subordinates impersonal; you do not have anybody looking over your shoulder telling you what you should do ... Muslims do not have an intermediary with God, there is no hierarchy, and they are not at ease with a boss who is on top of them, controlling them. With a procedure, they can self-check everything, and so they preserve their honour.

To sum up, even though Poulina's new management tools are highly influenced by the social regulation mechanisms one finds in the Tunisian context, such as the 'family' or 'craftsman' metaphors, their implementation did not take place spontaneously nor was it imposed from the top. The new aspects of the 'American' management techniques were subject to interpretation before being adopted and integrated in Poulina's management system. These new aspects received positive feedback from those involved only because the methods took on meaning within the Tunisian culture. Poulina's employees were willing to adhere to the new management style only because they felt treated in accordance with their ideal of a 'trustworthy' work relationship, as illustrated by the metaphors used in their accounts. The relational and procedural components of Poulina's management system limited its employees' actions in a way that respected their 'honour' and facilitated their acceptance of the company's objectives (Table 6.1).

DISCUSSION OF THE IMPLICATIONS FOR CROSS-CULTURAL MANAGEMENT

The Poulina case illustrates the importance of providing local and legitimate meanings to imported management techniques for successful implementation

Table 6.1 Poulina management: when American management system meets Tunisian management practices

	American management	Tunisian management	Poulins management
Features	'fair contract' ✔ Clearly defined contractual objectives ✔ Evaluation based on measurable indicators ✔ Control based on well-established facts	'a family based model' ✔ Few rules subject to interpretation ✔ Paternalistic leadership style ✔ Interference of personal relationships with working relations	'a big family with written rules' ✔ Contractual relationships to prevent the interference of personal relationships with working relations ✔ Written rules to 'guide' employees in improving their the performance
Implicit assumptions	Contracts freely negotiated between equals 'Mistrust of arbitrariness of the power'	Paternalism to overcome the humiliating situation of being subordinate 'Attachment to the values of equality and dignity'	A system that saves honour 'A craftsman is happier than a worker'

in developing countries. Employees' comments on Poulina's management practices indicated that they made sense of them via their local Tunisian cultural references rather than the 'American' meanings usually associated with these management practices in the USA. It is also notable that no evidence emerged suggesting a compromise between the two cultures.

The Poulina interviews suggest that local interpretations of American management techniques over the years have contributed to their acceptance. First, core aspects of the American management model, such as explicitness, clear goal-setting and formalization meet local needs for more 'rigour' and enable employees to limit personal relationships' interference with work. Second, the American management techniques are reinterpreted in connection with Tunisian cultural metaphors, for example, the craftsman as an independent entrepreneur: by using the craftsman analogy, employees respond to strict rules, but in autonomous ways. Though they remain in a subordinate relationship, they preserve their dignity and independence via strategies they adopt in response to strict rules.

Thus, far from making a trade-off between 'social ties' and 'rational organization', Poulina's implementation of new procedures succeeded because it echoed the ways Tunisian employees interpret social ties. One can find the same procedures everywhere, but how people assign meaning to them may vary from one country to another, leading to different framings of employees' roles. Poulina's employees used the craftsman analogy or the metaphor of the family, that is, recognizable social organization models in the Tunisian context, to make sense of the imported tools.

This case therefore challenges those who consider 'traditional aspects' of culture as self-evident obstacles to 'effective' management practices. It shows that culture provides more than a backdrop for applying universal tools: it supplies the terrain (ground) or 'grammar' that new techniques should integrate and deploy (Yousfi, 2007a). The chief lesson: culture can be seen as a resource, providing local and legitimate meanings to imported management techniques, as long as those techniques find harmonious readings within local frames of meaning. Once culture appears as a producer of meaning, the management practitioner's or scholar's tendency to assign it as immutable, inert or mechanical effects disappears. Culture comes into play in the modernization process primarily by giving specific meanings to management techniques (Yousfi, 2007b).

RECOMMENDATIONS FOR PRACTITIONERS

The aims of reformers concerned with modernizing management practices in developing countries (and the action programmes they adopt) do not exist independently of the reformers' own perception of the world. Their actions take on meaning, in their own eyes and those of the people they have to motivate, within a given structure of meanings. From this perspective, modernization's primary concern is no longer determining the best tools to ensure management effectiveness, but determining the relevant framework of meaning in each culture. It is this framework that will initiate effective management practices without compromising the locally shared conception of a 'good' relationship between individual autonomy and collective order.

Successful transfer of management techniques depends on giving a positive meaning to problematic situations by echoing positive experiences in the host society's framework of meaning. This requires organizing management practices so that modernization authentically reflects the local, legitimate conception of a well-ordered society. Such an approach looks beyond the resistance to imported tools that managers have encountered in some countries, and seeks to identify the resources each culture offers. It focuses less on the superiority of any particular model and more on how desired reforms become context-specific. Further research on gradual and successful contextualization may show exactly and concretely how 'universal' standards can best adapt to local contexts. Such an approach may lead to a new, more realistic and more effective view of management modernization approaches in developing countries.

NOTE

1. This research was funded by the French Development Agency.

REFERENCES

Agence Française de Devéloppement (AFD) (1998), *L'Afrique des entreprises. La Documentation Française,* Paris: AFD.
Boston Consulting Group (2010), 'The African challengers: global competitors emerge from the overlooked continent', available at http://www.bcg.com/documents/file44610.pdf, June (accessed 1 May 2010).
de Tocqueville, A. (1835), *Alexis de Tocqueville, De la démocratie en Amérique I,* Paris: Les Éditions Gallimard, reprinted 1992.
d'Iribarne, P. (1989), *La logique de l'honneur,* Paris: Seuil.
d'Iribarne, P., A. Henry, J.-P. Segal, S. Chevrier and T. Glokobar (1998), *Cultures et mondialisation,* Paris: Seuil.
d'Iribarne, P. (2009), 'Conceptualising national cultures: an anthropological perspective', *European Journal of International Manageeement,* 3(2), 167–75.
d'Iribarne, P. and A. Henry (2007), *Successful Companies in the Developing World: Managing in Synergy with Cultures,* Paris: Agence Française de Développement.
Foner, E. (1998), *The Story of American Freedom,* New York: W.W. Norton.
Geertz, C. (1973), *The Interpretation of Cultures,* New York: Basic Books.

Hofstede, G. (1980) *Culture's Consequences: International Differences in Work-related Values*, Beverly Hills, CA: Sage.

Leonard, D.K. (1987), 'The political realities of African management', *World Development*, **15**(7), 899–910.

Locke, J. (1980), Second treatise of government, US, C.B. Macpherson, originally published 1690.

Yousfi, H. (2007a), 'Culture and development: the continuing tension between modern standards and local contexts', Working Paper, Gestion et société, CNRS, Paris.

Yousfi, H. (2007b), 'Gérer en Jordanie: une coexistence problématique entre système hiérarchique et idéal religieux', *Revue Française de Gestion*, **33**(171), 157–173.

Yousfi, H. (2010), 'Culture and trust in contractual relationships: a French-Lebaneese cooperation', in M.N.K. Saunders, D. Skinner, G.Dietz, N. Gillespie and R.J. Lewicki (eds), *Organisational Trust: A Cultural Perspective*, Cambridge: Cambridge University Press, pp. 227–54.

Yousfi, H., E. Flipiake and H. Bougault (2005), *Poulina, un management tunisien*, Paris: Agence Française de Développement.

Zghal, R. (1989), *La culture de la dignité et le flou organisationnel: culture et comportement organisationnel, schéma théorique et application au cas tunisien*, Tunis: Centre d'étude de recherches et de publications.

7. Corporate communication across cultures: a multi-level approach

Lisbeth Clausen

INTRODUCTION

This chapter presents the study of the intercultural and cross-organizational challenges faced by a Danish company and its Japanese alliance partners. An examination of communication processes between headquarters and the subsidiary/alliance partner shows that the transmission model of communication is less suited to intercultural business settings than a model that involves co-creation of meaning and market. In this study, levels of cultural influence are divided into the global, the national, the professional and the individual levels. Each level influences communication processes. New understandings and cultural practices emerge, and these new ideas and approaches are ideally incorporated back into new corporate strategies. In this study the model is applied to the specific case of Denmark and Japan. It is equally applicable to the analysis of interaction between any headquarter and subsidiary/alliance.

The study is structured as follows. First, it presents corporate communication challenges of managers. Second, it presents conceptions of culture and communication to create a framework for a 'negotiated' culture perspective. Third, the methodology is presented in short. Fourth, the multi-level model is used to analyse strategic and operational communication between the Danish company and its Japanese subsidiary. Finally, the concluding sections present implications for practitioners and cross-cultural scholars.

CORPORATE COMMUNICATION CHALLENGES

All business activity involves communication. Within cross-cultural management, activities such as branding, leading, motivating, decision-making, problem-solving and exchanging ideas are all based on the ability of managers and employees from one culture to communicate successfully with colleagues, clients and suppliers from other cultures. Communicating effectively challenges managers even when working domestically with a culturally homogeneous workforce. When colleagues speak another language and come from a different cultural background, communication becomes considerably more difficult (Adler, 2002).

In a globalized business environment of increased complexity, most contemporary managers in cross-cultural communication believe that organizational existence hinges on the ability to establish and maintain the organization as a unified and integrated whole across different audiences. This belief increasingly shapes the communication strategies of corporations (Christensen et al., 2008). Many companies strive to integrate and streamline communications of business-related principles and values to various stakeholders from employees to customers throughout worldwide operations (Riusala et al., 2004). Standardizing the communication of corporate values and strategic practices is perceived as one of the central prerequisites of success (Szulanski, 2003). The use of standardized codes of conduct is one example of how corporate values are integrated and streamlined (see Chapter 5).

Nevertheless, in spite of global standardization processes, local cultural factors, as demonstrated in this study and in the other chapters of this volume, still influence the adaptation of strategies and practices at the local level. Our study concerns the collaboration and communication between a Danish corporation's headquarters and its subsidiary in Japan. A multi-level analysis provides examples of how managers perceive and process information and how they communicate messages with people in a bicultural setting. Although it was clear that professional values move business forward, the cultural dimension was an important factor at every level of the analysis: culture is negotiated in every business encounter (Brannen and Salk, 2000; Clausen, 2007).

CONCEPTIONS OF CULTURE AND COMMUNICATION

Managers identify and affiliate with a multiplicity of values, the meanings of which are continually being negotiated depending on the contextual influences of their encounters. To capture the complexity in interaction, the present study employs a social constructivist view (Blasco and Gustafsson, 2003; Søderberg and Holden, 2002) in which culture is something that is mutually constructed among participants and depends on context (Sackmann and Phillips, 2004). A social constructivist perspective defines culture as 'shared or partly shared patterns of meaning and interpretation [which] … are produced, reproduced and continually changed by the people identifying with them and negotiating them' (Søderberg and Holden, 2002, p. 112).

A multi-level model is employed to capture the dynamics of intercultural encounters and the processes of globalization and change from macro to micro levels. It is based on the concept of 'emerging culture' or 'negotiated culture' (Brannen and Salk, 2000, p. 451; Clausen, 2007). Thus, the role of individuals and their influence on communication are seen as contributing to the formation of new cultural norms and rules for interaction, which then become part of a 'negotiated and emergent culture' (Brannen and Salk, 2000). Further, while culture is understood as negotiated in different contextual settings, communication is understood as dialogic and reflective. Interpretations and meanings hence are plentiful or 'polyphonic' (Cornelissen, 2008).

METHODOLOGY

The study is based on interviews with 50 employees in five companies at all levels, ranging from directors and managers from human resources, culture and communications, branding, merchandizing and marketing to operational staff and trainees in Denmark and Japan (Clausen, 2006). This chapter presents the case of a company that allocates a vast amount of resources in aligning corporate values and standardizing communication and activities across borders. The interviews were semi-structured and lasted from one to three hours (Kvale, 1996). The approach is grounded (Glaser and Strauss, 1967) and empirically bound (taking the point of departure in lessons learned by managers). I spent time in the Danish and Japanese organizations to get a feel for both the people and their practices (Kvale, 1996; Van Maanen, 1988). I subsequently returned to present findings to the managers I had interviewed. Some of their feedback is included in this chapter.

THE MULTI-LEVEL MODEL

The following presents the lessons learned at the Danish company concerning communication with their Japanese subsidiary – and vice versa. The analysis is organized systematically following the multi-level communication model (see Figure 7.1). The 'global' level relates to the corporate global communication strategies and images and their reception in Japan. The 'national' level refers to the corporate cultural values that have influenced the considerations and strategies of the operations of the company in Japan. The 'organizational' level demonstrates the organization of communication processes. It shows how Danish and Japanese national values, as well as corporate cultural values, affect communication. The 'professional' level presents the communication of professional (departmental) knowledge including product-specific information. Finally, the 'individual' level highlights intercultural competence and experience in business communication and relationship building in bicultural contexts.

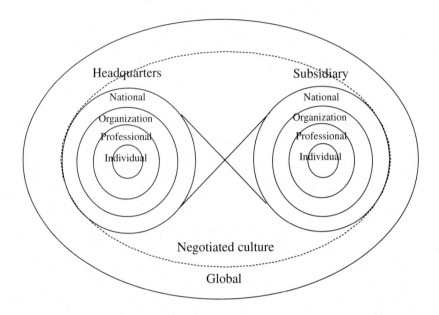

Source: Clausen (2006), reprinted with permission.

*Figure 7.1   The multi-level communication model, influences on managers
                in intercultural encounters: global, national, organizational,
                professional and individual levels*

CASE: THE AUDIO-VISUAL COMPANY (AV COMPANY)

The AV Company was founded in 1925. It currently has 2500 employees, and
its annual turnover is 548.6 million euros. It is listed on the Copenhagen Stock
Exchange. It is present in more than one hundred countries with 1200 stores
around the world, of which approximately 65 per cent exclusively sell its products. The AV Company sells high-quality audio-visual products and exclusive
sound.

The Global Level

Each level in the model exemplifies communication and cultural challenges.
The global level shows how the corporate effort to standardize branding and
image creation meets challenges at the local level with regard to cultural issues
in distribution and human resource in the re-establishment process.

The AV Company uses global branding strategies and standardized tools for image creation in its markets. The global marketing platform is situated in London, and from there activities are coordinated worldwide. The company first entered the Tokyo market in the 1960s and operated through different entry modes, from importers and agents to its own subsidiary. While the agent and importer contracts were not a good match, they were necessary stepping stones on the way to implementing the company's chosen strategy in Japan. In the year 2000, a wholly owned subsidiary was established for the second time in Tokyo to regain full control of the brand. The cultural challenge of building a new subsidiary business team was a long and 'uphill battle', according to the regional director. In reasserting their control of the operation in Japan, the AV Company started from a long period (of seven years) without growth. The brand had been diluted by their former agent's short-term strategy, and this had to be turned around in the new wholly owned subsidiary. The overall decision to re-establish a sales and marketing subsidiary in Japan was only reached after many years of hard work and discord between the operating team in Japan and the corporate headquarters in Denmark.

As part of the strategy to standardize the global brand image, retail outlets in Japan were reduced from 10 000 different stores to 200 brand and shop-in-shops. This was not easily accomplished due to the traditional Japanese *jinmyaky* system of conducting business through longstanding connections. The fact that results improved drastically during the subsidiary's first year was exceptional, particularly considering the fact that it typically takes much longer to engineer a successful turnaround in Japan. While business results were successful, coordinating different working styles was a big challenge in the turnaround. As expressed by the regional manager, 'It is not possible to set an exact date for the transformation, but it took about three years.' After three years, it was clear that the more entrepreneurial AV Company spirit had prevailed, although to this day in Japan it must be tempered with a respect for the relationship-building that is a part of traditional Japanese business practices. Some relationships and business networks remained with a number of employees who transferred from the importer to the new subsidiary. Ultimately, 'a culture which is seventy to eighty percent new' has emerged, and the regional manager considers this progress a success. In his opinion, it is one thing to turn around the financial situation, as this simply requires market knowledge, capable execution and hard work. Cultural transformation, however, is another matter altogether, as it requires a deep understanding of both cultures: 'The culture you operate in and the culture you wish to infuse … It was a long walk', according to the regional manager. The strategy from headquarters was to create a common platform of communication by 'infusing' strong corporate values ('DNA'), as described below.

The global level of analysis, therefore, demonstrates ongoing tensions between headquarters and the local management concerning strategic business aims, which over time resulted in a new business structure in Japan. A number of employees from the early set-up have transferred to the new team, thus becoming carriers and negotiators of both the old and the new cultures.

The National Level

The AV Company culture is grounded in the countryside of Denmark inside high-tech glass buildings. Outside the modern factory, natural abundance hosts a large dairy industry, plenty of wheat fields and beaches. A substantial portion of the administrative staff comes from the surrounding area, while engineers are recruited nationwide. While it is difficult to measure just how much the AV Company culture is influenced by the surrounding mentality, according to the regional manager, the AV corporate culture is unique. In fact, he sees it almost as a religion:

> The best that we can do is to educate and train our staff so that they become dedicated evangelists. If you want to be a Muslim you go to Mecca. If you want to be a Catholic you go to Rome. And if you want to be a true AV Company employee, you go to … [HQ]. Here you become transfused with the right blood as if by osmosis. You meet all the company heroes that are part of our corporate culture, from the creative designers to the people on the factory floor who produce the products for you to sell.

According to the regional manager, the AV Company management cherishes the feeling of being 'one big family', and 'it feels good to be where it all started and where it is still going on'. He finds the experience of a visit to be an important source of knowledge for employees who work outside Denmark and a critical part of their becoming an 'ambassador' for the brand. 'The more of a transfusion you have had from HQ, the more convincing and credible you will sound', he said. The whole experience leads to a professionalism and dedication that are essential when talking about the brand to both retail partners and customers. According to the regional manager, when the retail staff from Japan are sent to Denmark for a week of training, their sales go up when they return because they have stories to tell. It is therefore important to train employees with the objective of creating a shared organizational history and background. All of these objectives are enhanced by the regular visits, as well as the daily phone and internet communication that takes place across the distance separating the two organizations.

Questioning the ordinary – global vision
The vision statement of AV Company is: 'Courage to constantly question the ordinary in search of surprising long lasting experiences.' This is a very

powerful statement, according to the regional manager: 'You can read it again and again, and it is actually embodied in everything that we do. We want to challenge the ordinary. We want to be different, and we want to create these magical experiences and surprises.'

The mission statement, the brand identity value and the core competence areas form a 'three-layer rocket' that encompasses the soul of the AV Company (the brand identity values are performance, design, humanization, craftsmanship; the core competence areas are quality, picture, sound, user interaction, design, integration, mechanical movements, materials and finish, as cited on the homepage). While the products themselves, in the view of the regional manager, are the end result of what the AV Company employees do, the characteristics of these products both influence and are influenced by the employee behaviour and creative mentality that lie behind their creation. In this sense, the 'concept value chain' goes all the way from the employees, through the products, to the end customer. This is the primary reason why knowledge of the core values is critical, and why they are emphasized in employee training aimed at spreading and strengthening the AV Company corporate culture.

In interviews at the Tokyo office, a number of managers mentioned 'questioning the ordinary'. However, according to the Japanese marketing manager, this phrase does not necessarily promote a desirable image in the Japanese culture. On the contrary, being similar (ordinary) and blending in are virtues for most Japanese. So, although the concept is ingrained as a form of knowledge in the employees' heads, it does not have the same marketing effects in Japan as it may have in Denmark or elsewhere.

As we have seen, meaning is often culturally bound, and the ultimate interpretation of many of the values may change, even significantly, in the Japanese context.

The Organizational Level

To motivate employees and to mediate between the Danish corporate headquarters and the Japanese organization in the Tokyo office, two organizational charts were used for the division of tasks and responsibilities. One chart shows the formal hierarchy of the organization, and the other shows a matrix of responsibilities.

The first chart indicates the titles and reporting structure of the organization. This is important to the Japanese staff because status and place in the hierarchy influence their sense of commitment and behaviour. However, according to the regional manager, this traditional organizational chart does not indicate how the organization actually works and what the daily tasks are. He preferred the matrix configuration. However, in his experience it was quite radical to present this matrix when he was in charge of the Tokyo office because it does not show who reports to whom, nor does it pay attention to organizational hierarchy. He soon learned from his employees that the hierarchy and the number of years that someone has been with the company are of great importance. The matrix does not identify the managers, which was very confusing for the Japanese staff. Therefore, both charts are displayed on the whiteboard in the office so that everyone knows who manages whom. In the view of the regional director, the matrix 'highlights the core business functions, as well as where the money is'. While he was fond of his 'dynamic', matrix organizational chart, the 12 office members preferred the linear organizational chart. Thus, the organization charts symbolize both the Danish egalitarian and straightforward business culture and the more traditional hierarchical Japanese ways of thinking.

The observations at the organizational level thus display the differences in management expectations and show that parallel practices based on organizational culture exist and are continuously negotiated.

The Professional Level

Negotiation of ideas is not only influenced by the different national values of the country of origin; sometimes professional, that is, departmental, goals also influence communication. According to the Japanese marketing manager: 'Financial managers are oriented towards numerical bottom lines, and people like myself are creative people working with emotional bottom lines in their branding efforts. We often experience a communication gap' (Japanese marketing manager, interview November 2004).

Additionally, from the Japanese view there are several product-specific challenges in working with Scandinavian management and a Scandinavian brand. According to the Japanese marketing manager, AV Company customers have a difficult time even pronouncing the brand name, and few people in the population at large even know where Denmark is. However, she finds that the professional similarities to her previous positions (with European and American luxury brands) are greater than the differences. The simplicity that characterizes the lifestyles and design of the Danes and the Japanese is a common cultural trait – and a likeable and sellable one:

> Although the AV Company is far away from us physically, their mentality is familiar and close. Danish cultural traditions include simplicity, which allows us as Japanese to feel close to Danish culture and the Danish people. Simplicity is a common denominator. People who discover the AV Company's characteristics feel comfortable with the products and the aesthetics of the design.

Not surprisingly, however, some business practices and ideas are new to her. While the AV Company is promoted as an upscale brand in Denmark, for instance, she targets an even more exclusive image in Japan. The AV Company is being promoted as an aspirational brand in an effort to reach the Japanese elite. In addition to a number of activities each year, the AV Company contributes to the creation of an exclusive, glamorous book for their 2000 top clients. This book initiative exemplifies the local branding effort particular to Japan. She cooperates with nine companies to build a brand community with customers. The customers have a high disposable income, a Western-oriented lifestyle and are open to non-Japanese products and technology. 'The Japanese are extremely interested in what is behind the product. They want to know about the core values of the companies, the corporate history and the origin of key ideas. They want the story of the efforts we put into creating unique product concepts' (Regional manager).

Previously, the AV Company was unable to deliver a constant flow of new product developments in response to consumer demands, as requested by the Tokyo office. Consequently, alternative and unique efforts, such as the co-branding initiative, were accepted by headquarters. In other instances, the Danish mentality concerning marketing is not always as upbeat as needed in the buzzing brand centre of Tokyo.

The professional level shows how functional specialists may be challenged with national cultural issues concerning consumer preferences and market demands, as well as how they are challenged to negotiate between numerical and creative bottom-lines. While the analytical levels above concern professional knowledge and its influence on communication, the next level is connected to the degree of internationalization of mindset.

The Individual Level

Starting again in 2000 with a wholly owned subsidiary, establishing a capable team was a lengthy process. The startup period was filled with many positive and negative aspects of human resource management. Four elements were considered to be important employee characteristics in setting up a new team: attitude (sensitivity), gender, language and experience. 'Sensitivity is one of the main elements in intercultural competence', according to the regional director (who is Danish but fluent in the Japanese language and referred to as 'ethnic Japanese' by his Tokyo staff). His strongest tool in maintaining the corporate culture is to hire people who are sensitive and able to internalize company beliefs: 'You cannot control culture and you should not try to, but if you hire people who are fundamentally in agreement with you and the company values, you are on the right track.'

How is this done in the new organization in Japan? Two out of three managers are female, which is not unusual within foreign-owned companies in Japan. According to the regional manager, expatriates commonly acknowledge the numerous advantages of recruiting Japanese women. (A fourth manager never fit into the new organization, in large part because his new superior was younger than him and female.) In the regional manger's view, Japanese women are generally 'efficient, culturally intelligent and higher performing than the men'. Also, staff with bicultural (Japanese-Western) experience is preferred. An important responsibility of the office manager, for instance, is to be a mediator between the AV Company in Denmark and the office in Japan. Her communication activities vary from being international, European or Danish to 'being very conservatively Japanese'. The conservative mode of interaction is used with Japanese customers: 'One way to think about my role is that of an interpreter. I have to know about the European and the Japanese ways of doing things. Knowledge of one culture is not enough.'

Language, she says, does not only mean English or Japanese, which of course are the common means of communication. It also means professional or personal language. Although she speaks English fluently and has many years of experience abroad as well as in European companies, she encounters problems of understanding between people who are from different professional backgrounds. She employs people with English competence and encourages her office staff to improve their English skills, but finds that international understanding only comes after many years of experience in an international and professional environment.

The individual level shows the particular company strategies concerning staffing in Japan. Knowledge of both Danish and Japanese business cultures is an advantage, and sensitivity enhances the ability to handle different cultural values.

In summary, the use of the multi-level communication model shows how managers are influenced by a multiplicity of factors at every level of encounters. The use of the model shows that meanings are not just adopted but transformed, changed – in short, negotiated.

RECOMMENDATIONS TO PRACTITIONERS

This study illustrates that in spite of the fact that globalization processes force managers to adopt strategies of standardization and homogenization of practices and products, local cultural factors still influence the adaptation of strategies and practices. To get their messages across in this setting, managers have to be experts in their industrial and professional fields as well as aware of the national and organizational context and the backgrounds of their counterparts. Cultural encounters may include professional aspects of communication concerning product marketing and image creation, market entry, the organization of communication as well as task-related issues. Some of the learning points across levels based on the manager's quotes were:

- Global messages do not automatically mean local acceptance.
- Creating a brand (making that difference based on local catch phrases) is important.
- Cultural transformation requires a deep understanding of both cultures: the culture you operate in and the culture you wish to infuse.
- Cultural differences are not a valid excuse for failure: 'You cannot do this. In Japan it does not work ...' (You can – you just have to find the way.) 'You cannot do this in Denmark' is equally an invalid excuse.
- If you don't become a strong brand in Japan relatively quickly your time there will be limited.
- Business ways can be learned – culture is the real science.
- Cultural competence is when you compare with things Japanese rather than with things from your own country.
- People matter. Competencies and culture deserve attention.

The learning points show that managers from two very distinct national and organizational cultures were able to meet and incorporate experience from their cultural encounters over time and evolve 'negotiated' cultures. In the bicultural relationships of Danish and Japanese managers as presented, managers from both sides expressed a high awareness of their own national (and organizational) cultures. It was found that the ability to change perceptions enabled reflection and the accumulation of new knowledge. It was also found that although managers, just like the rest of us, tend to be content to remain in their (mental) cultural comfort-zones, managers who operate successfully across boarders are able to apply their cultural knowledge in practice.

CONCLUSION

In theory the multi-level contextual model offers a glimpse of the complexity of intercultural encounters in headquarter-alliance communication. Findings support previous research stating that managers may enter intercultural situations with certain mindsets based on national, professional and organizational cultural values, and that a new situation-specific culture then emerges based on contextual influences and task-related factors (Brannen and Salk, 2000). It was exemplified how culture is 'negotiated' through ongoing communication by organizational members. Factors from each contextual level may influence communication processes as described above. New understandings and cultural practices emerge, and these new ideas and approaches are ideally incorporated back into new corporate strategies. For truly cross-cultural management strategies to triumph, it is necessary for intercultural businesses to overcome communication gaps and cultural 'translation' difficulty and learn to successfully incorporate the local into the global.

REFERENCES

Adler, N.J. (2002), *The International Dimension of Organizational Behavior*, 4th edn, Cincinnati, OH: South-Western.

Blasco, M. and J. Gustafsson (2003), *Intercultural Alternatives. Critical Perspectives on Intercultural Encounters in Theory and Practice*, Copenhagen: Copenhagen Business School Press.

Brannen, M.Y. and J.E. Salk (2000), 'Partnering across boarders: negotiating organizational culture in a German-Japanese joint venture', *Human Relations*, **53**(4), 451–87.

Clausen, L. (2006), 'Display 24. The multilevel communication model, influences on managers in intercultural encounters: global, national, organisational, professional and individual levels', in *Intercultural Organisational Communication. Five Corporate Cases in Japan*, Copenhagen: Copenhagen Business School Press, p. 65.

Clausen, L. (2007), 'Corporate communication challenges: a "negotiated" culture perspective', *International Journal of Cross Cultural Management*, **7**(3), 317–32.

Christensen, L.T., M. Morsing and G. Cheney (2008), *Corporate Communications: Convention, Challenge, Complexity*, London: Sage.

Cornelissen, J.P. (2008), *Corporate Communications. A Guide to Theory and Practice*, 2nd edn, London: Sage.

Glaser, B.G. and A.L. Strauss (1967), *The Discovery of Grounded Theory: Strategies for Qualitative Research*, Chicago, OH: Aldine.

Kvale, S. (1996), *InterViews: An Introduction to Qualitative Research Interviewing*, Thousand Oaks, CA: Sage.

Riusala, K. and V. Suutari (2004), 'International knowledge transfers through expatriates', *Thunderbird International Business Review*, **46**(6), 743–70.

Sackmann, S.A. and M.E. Phillips (2004), 'Contextual influences on culture research: shifting assumptions for new workplace realities', *International Journal of Cross-Cultural Management*, **4**(3), 370–90.

Søderberg, A.-M. and N. Holden (2002), 'Rethinking cross cultural management in a globalizing business world', *International Journal of Cross-Cultural Management*, **2**(1), 103–21.

Szulanski, G. (2003), *Sticky Knowledge Barriers to Knowing in the Firm*, London: Sage.

Van Maanen, J. (1988), *Tales of the Field: On Writing Ethnography*, Chicago, IL: University of Chicago Press.

8. Engineering culture(s) across sites: implications for cross-cultural management of emic meanings

Jasmin Mahadevan

INTRODUCTION

Cultural difference in organizations is often referred to as national cultural difference. Yet as culture provides a focus point for collective belonging, it can also be conceptualized as 'collective identity', a direction this chapter is going to follow. Collective identities can develop on different levels, even if different aspects of culture, for example, artefacts, might be shaped by an organization's national cultural surroundings. This suggests that organizations are made up of more than mere national cultural identities – we can also find professional cultures, organizational cultures and site culture, to only name a few.

It is often suggested that these alternate collective identities are mere 'subcultures' and hence of lesser importance than national cultural differences. However, from the anthropological point of view, all levels of collective identity can and might be equally powerful – depending, for example, on context, plays of power, individual or group agenda. Using the case of a German high-tech company and its offshore site in India, this chapter will show when and how these alternative collective identities become salient. For the sake of confidentiality, all names have been changed.

THEORETICAL BACKGROUND AND METHOD

Culture is many things, depending on perspective. However, to understand the findings from this case, one has to look at culture anthropologically, and this is the reason for the first section of this chapter to be devoted to theory.

Recent anthropological theory since Geertz (1973) conceptualizes culture as an open process of sense-making in interaction with changing boundaries. This making of a collective 'We' always takes place in interaction with the making of a group of 'Other' (Ricoeur, 1992). Perception of collective 'Self' and 'Other', inside (emic) and outside (etic) views on cultural discourse usually differ from each other. For the study of culture this means: Whom actors in the field perceive as different might, and most likely will, differ from expected difference from the outside view.

To uncover these emic views on collective identities, fieldwork has become the method of choice in organizational anthropology. Fieldwork essentially relies on the researcher to go into the field, to live with the actors and learn to live like them. On the one hand, fieldworkers participate, on the other hand, they observe action and actors from a higher stance. Through constant participant observation and reflexive practice researchers are drawn into a relationship between researcher and field which they keep track of through constant field notes. Thus, researchers themselves are the main tool of research and analysis.

For this case, two years of fieldwork were conducted in the field. The field was divided into the primary field, that is, the technical department to be researched, and the secondary field, that is, other corporate departments such as human resources that interacted with the primary field.

Data in the primary field was collected through initial interviews with 15 key actors and subsequent participant observation over two years (18 months at the German site, six weeks at the Indian site), including approximately 250 formal and informal interviews with members from three sites. After six months of research a core group of 31 key actors was identified. Interpretations were constantly mirrored back to the field and discussed with key actors in focus sessions until agreed upon to establish inter-subjectivity.

Data in the secondary field was collected through 34 days of participant observations of workshops, 36 qualitative semi-structured and 50 informal interviews. Additionally, I relied on cultural documents such as internal information distributed by corporate communications and corporate press releases and information spread by the media.

CASE PRESENTATION: CHIP-TECH CORPORATION

The field is a German designer and manufacturer of micro-chips, to be called ChipTech Corporation. ChipTech can look back on more than 100 years of organizational history. Its headquarters are located in Stadt, one of the major cities in Germany.

Approximately 20 years ago, corporate internationalization began. At the beginning of the twenty-first century, the company has approximately 8000 employees in Germany and 35 000 worldwide. During the time of the research, approximately 15 per cent of the employees in Stadt were non-German nationals, mainly from other European countries. The official corporate language was German.

Virtually every ChipTech employee has an engineering degree, mainly a Master of Science (that is, the German degree called 'diplom'), mainly in electrical engineering or computer science, depending on the task at hand. In research and development departments, one third of the employees have even completed a doctorate in these fields.

I will call this highly qualified technical workforce 'engineers' which is also the name they give themselves. As several authors have shown, engineering communities can be viewed as a transnational and de-localized community of experts with global, partly virtual practices that are considered to be highly universal (Gupta and Ferguson, 1997; Mahadevan, 2009).

During the time of the research, ChipTech ramped up an offshore site in the Indian town of Puram, mainly to realize the advantages of low labour costs. The corporate unit that was responsible for the ramp-up in Puram is the primary field of this case. It is to be called Technical Unit (TU). During the time of the research, TU consisted of approximately 450 members at three major sites, that is, the German central headquarters (approximately 250 members), a site in France (approximately 60 members) and a site in India (approximately 140 members at peak).

The purpose of TU: engineers from all three sites developed a complex, interdependent and distributed technological system that was to be used by internal customers for improvement of microchip design. Thus, TU is an internal department, located between service and research and development. Its customers are those ChipTech units that develop microchips which is the purpose of ChipTech organization. All TU managers had a degree in software or electrical engineering; I will therefore call them 'engineering managers'.

The secondary field of research was other company departments such as human resources (HR) and external providers of intercultural training who were employed by HR. These so-called central departments are the only departments that are headed by non-engineering managers and staffed with people without an engineering degree. I will therefore call members of these departments 'non-engineering managers'.

From the actors' perspective, the ramp-up of the Indian site constituted a major organizational and cultural change. Uncertainty was aggravated by profound reorganization – called 'the reorganization' by employees – that started shortly after the ramp-up decision had been made and threatened the existence of TU and thus influenced the cross-site work practice tremendously. It was feared by virtually every employee that 'the reorganization' in the end might make them superfluous. Parallel to these insecure boundary conditions, TU employees were required to transfer knowledge to India and build up expertise over there.

CASE ANALYSIS: COLLECTIVE IDENTITIES IN THE FIELD

Dominant Discourses

Dominant etic discourse: national cultural identity

Regarding national culture, non-engineering managers in the secondary field of HR thought this concept to be of paramount importance to cross-site engineering work practice, more precisely to have a negative impact on it. Their firm belief could be summarized as: 'National cultural difference exists and it does harm cross-site work.' When the site in Puram was ramped up, non-engineering managers expected engineers to have 'cross-cultural issues' due to differences in religion, customs, tradition and etiquette between 'Germany' and 'India' – regardless, for example, of the fact that more than 15 nationalities were working together at TU in Germany – often communicating in English.

At the same time, non-engineering managers thought of engineers as being socially and thus interculturally incompetent. Hence, they expected engineers to have 'intercultural' issues in the national cultural sense. One company HR manager said: 'They [the engineers] simply don't have enough social skills – and how should they, considering the kind of work they do!'

This view on technical employees as being socially less competent due to the (technical) nature of their work is a common view held by non-engineering employees. Dahlén (1997, p. 1) has called this phenomenon a 'packaging of knowledge'. According to Dahlén this packaging serves two purposes: on the one hand, it alienates supposedly foreign cultures, on the other hand, it also legitimizes the cross-cultural manager's claim to competence, for they are the only ones who can overcome this difference. To summarize Dahlén's point: cross-cultural managers (he calls them 'interculturalists') need to first construct foreign cultures as 'alien' in order to make their own knowledge on cultural difference indispensable for the organization. If the Indian engineer were no different from the German one, then the cross-cultural manager and their knowledge would be superfluous.

The main interaction between TU and HR during the time of the research was through intercultural training activities: HR made it mandatory for every TU manager and project leader to attend a two-day intercultural training on India, Germany or France (or a combination of two of these countries). This training focused on national cultural difference. It worked with the intercultural dimensions of Hofstede (1980, 2003) and Trompenaars and Hampden-Turner (1997) and pointed out the national cultural differences between these countries. It did acknowledge the presence of subcultures but merely mentioned them on a slide. When I observed one of these training sessions, a mere eight minutes of two full working days was spent on the topic of professional subcultures.

Dominant emic discourse: professional identity

From the engineering perspective (meaning engineers and engineering management), culture was categorized as 'national culture' too. Yet only a few members of TU believed 'culture' in the sense of 'national culture' to have an influence on engineering work-practice. Culture in general was perceived as something outside one's own work practice. As one engineer (himself of German nationality) describes another engineer (of Indian nationality): 'He is not Indian. I know Vinod since four years, he is an expert in his topic, he is simply a colleague to me; we talk technically to each other.' An Indian engineer at the Indian site said: 'On the street, Germans don't speak English – at work, people do speak English because this is the language of engineering.' This can be interpreted as a firm belief in engineering as a global profession that is not impacted by national cultural difference.

When members of the secondary field – non-engineering managers – would hear of such statements, they would categorize it as a proof for lack of social skills among engineers and intensify their intercultural training programme efforts. Hence, they interpreted the engineers' belief in engineering as a global profession as a rejection of national cultural difference.

Following Bennett's (1986) model of intercultural learning, rejection of national cultural difference could indeed by interpreted as the ethnocentric stage of 'minimalization' in intercultural learning. According to Bennett (1986), most intercultural learners will first negate and then minimize national cultural difference before they can then fully acknowledge difference. The full acknowledgement of difference is seen by Bennett as a prerequisite for trying out alternative roles, changing one's own role and incorporating other cultures into one's own values and behaviour.

However, if one follows the anthropological approach and tries to uncover emic discourses, one has to discard Bennett's model as an etic one. The anthropological demand goes one step further: How it really is, is of no consequence for culture is made and shaped by actors through their own imagination and sense-making in interaction. In that sense, objective reality does not exist. Any intercultural training activity should thus focus on uncovering emic perspectives and not objective truth.

From the emic perspective, the respective other to engineers is not 'the German' or 'the Indian', it is 'management'. Or, as engineering managers and engineers during times of crisis often commented: 'Luckily enough, we have not yet reached the stage where people like you [that is, people without an engineering degree] can become manager at ChipTech.' Or they would say: 'No wonder that [bad thing] is happening: we simply have too many non-engineering people managing the company.' If one truly takes the emic perspectives first, then any intercultural training activity for engineers would need to incorporate cultural discourses on the management-engineering difference for more than mere eight minutes in two days.

Frontstage versus backstage integration

Based on Kunda (1992), qualitative studies of engineering practice have viewed the engineering-management conflict in technical companies as given. Two reasons are that, first, from the anthropological perspective, engineers strive for technological freedom to realize the best-possible technological solution. Management control thwarts this goal which makes it likely that engineers might resist. Second, in this situation, engineers are a dangerous other for management, for they possess superior knowledge and thus cannot be fully controlled. Hence, their resistance is likely to be successful.

However, if this conflict was omnipresent in technical companies, one could ask from an anthropological perspective: how can the organization function? Again, it is not the purpose to judge how the system 'organization' could function better from a management perspective but to uncover how actors do make it function according to their own rules.

Goffman's (1959) notion of play and his differentiation of contexts into 'frontstage' and 'backstage' can be of help here. 'Frontstage', two groups in interaction will behave in line with expected collective behaviour. Very often, interaction of such a kind is ritualized, thus not to be analysed for its content but for its symbolic purpose. 'Real' interaction for content will take place elsewhere, that is, offstage: Here, individuals from two parties can cooperate even though their official roles demand for ritualized conflict between these two parties onstage. This means: every analysis of 'real' cross-cultural issues within a company has to take context into account.

At TU, engineers and engineering managers would routinely contradict each other in meetings at which I participated. Scheduled meetings between two groups are a frontstage scenario. Whenever a manager would suggest a change in the schedule, specification or project planning, project leaders and engineers would answer with 'this is not possible', 'this impacts functionality, 'this will be the end of the whole project', 'this will not work', 'even if we deliver it, we cannot guarantee functionality under such circumstances', 'you only think about cost-reduction, and you sacrifice technology for it' and many more. In all meetings I observed on matters such as project planning, schedule and specification, discussions on such matters would end without agreement.

After the end of the meeting, however, engineers and managers would continue to discuss the matter informally, often in front of the coffee-machine or over lunch. This is a classical backstage scenario. There, managers would use phrases such as 'well, you know, I used to be an engineer, too, I know how it is like' and engineers would use phrases such as 'yes, I know ...'. During all backstage interaction I observed, in the end, an agreement was found and carried out – until the next meeting. With the help of Goffman and the anthropological perspective, this dialogue can be interpreted as the following: backstage, engineering managers construct themselves as 'engineers, too', and are acknowledged by engineers.

Therefore, I interpreted management-engineering frontstage interaction as ritualized symbolic contradiction that was to be integrated backstage. The main means of backstage integration was the hybrid quality of engineering-management's identity: having an engineering background themselves, they can switch back to an alternate identity.

Unfortunately, as HR was an external department, most interaction between TU and HR took place frontstage. Therefore, HR non-engineering managers did not have access to backstage discourses of collective identity at TU. Thus, to them, frequent contradiction by engineers was just another proof for engineers not having social competencies. As one HR manager said: 'You can't even have a structured meeting with these people [the engineers]! How are we supposed to teach them advanced intercultural competency!'

Contextual Discourses of Defence and Appeasement

If etic and emic views on culture differ, one might ask: what then creates the real problems in engineering across sites at ChipTech? Unfortunately, this question cannot be answered easily, for it lies at the heart of every categorization of collective identity that it is influenced by the opposing categorization of the 'Other' as well as changing boundary conditions. For analysis of collective identity in organizations, personal feelings of endangerment, consecutive strategies of defence and counter-strategies of appeasement are of paramount importance.

For TU this means: when it comes to organizational power, an engineer depends on other engineers' knowledge. A new engineer in Puram depends on the German engineers' willingness and ability to transfer adequate knowledge to him. Otherwise, the new engineer will not be enabled to work 'as a good engineer'. At the same time, both engineers and managers have to be placed in the context of the organization at large: will there be, for example, employment reduction in Germany due to transfer of knowledge to India? If the German employees have the feeling that they might lose their job due to re-organization after having transferred their knowledge to the new site in India they might develop counter-strategies to prevent this. Their sense of being endangered or not thus lies at the very heart of the strategy they might choose.

How fear of losing one's job can influence knowledge transfer among an engineering community can be best illustrated by quoting Indian perspectives on the German site. Let's start with Anil, aged 27. He has been working for TU for 18 months. Anil remembers being sent to Stadt for initial training after his first days in Puram:

> [In Stadt], I got the feeling: 'They are afraid of losing their job.' For example, this colleague of mine, he sat down with us during lunch and started talking about his expectations. And there was a lot about this: 'What is going to happen to us?' Stadt-people are not very happy about Puram and this kind of stuff.

So, Anil clearly sees fear of change and loss of employment at the German site. Yet does this boundary condition influence individual strategy? Another Puram engineer, Karthik, aged 25, and a fairly new member of TU, talks about the following recent episode in working together with the German site. He says:

> Martin, he is an engineer in the Stadt-team. He was formerly doing my job, but then it became clear that this was going to be assigned to me, and that his responsibilities were going to shift. So I took his code and started testing it, and he was excellent support to me, and it used to be a jolly conversation, he always was very open with me.
>
> After some time, he send me some code he had written and told me: 'Give it a good shape.' And I found many bugs in the code and I made an Excel Sheet, nice and clean. It was a big list, stating: These were the bugs, and that's what we did about them. And I send it out to him via e-mail along with a documentation of how we improved the code, saying: 'please review'. And then there was no reaction.
>
> And some days later, Michael [another colleague from Stadt] told me that Martin had said: 'I won't talk to these people again.' And, you know, we only wanted to improve the usability of that code, we only wanted to improve the tool and the project. And this was really strange, you know; all the time you have this image in mind of Germans being very straightforward and very non-emotional and you are also told to work exactly like that: non-emotional, high-quality and all those pictures you have in mind when it comes to German engineering.

Very clearly, Karthik refers to organizational power here: simply because he is new, he might not speak up to the established expert. Karthik even has a clear understanding of German national culture, he knows that non-emotionality and straightforward, facts-oriented approaches are highly valued. Yet in this case, due to boundary conditions that from Martin's perspective aggravate uncertainty, he cannot succeed with this strategy. What did Karthik do? He continues:

> So, what we then did, was: We had two meetings with Martin just to make him feel comfortable again – there was no other purpose behind these meetings – and we explained what we thought and asked for his opinion and so on and so on, and slowly he was back to normal.
>
> See, this is how it is: When some Stadt-guy finds 100 bugs in my code and sends back just an Excel Sheet and tells me: 'In Stadt, it's just like that, we don't fuss

about personal feelings, we just state technical facts nice and clear', then I have to live with it, whatever I may feel. But on the other hand, if I do it the same Stadt-way, technically only, nice and clear, then people feel they have the right to take it personally because I am only the stupid Indian computer-*wallah* [*wallah* is a person who does something] who doesn't know a thing.

Again, Karthik refers to organizational power here: being treated as an inferior *wallah* seems to annoy him very much. Furthermore, this quote shows that he did choose an alternate strategy of appeasement in the end, a strategy that minimized fear from Martin's side. As soon as fear was minimized, global engineering identity took place again, or as Karthik put it: 'slowly he [Martin] was back to normal'. It is also important to note that Karthik, like all other engineers talking about each other, does not call people from the other sites 'Germans' but 'Stadt-people'. This clearly indicates that from the engineering perspective, distance and not national culture is what separates engineers.

A few weeks after having heard of this incident, I talked to the German engineer Martin, aged 53 and working for ChipTech for 32 years. He says:

Working together with Puram is uncertain. I don't know what will happen to me afterwards. What will my expertise be afterwards? But it will not be worse for me; it will be worse for the company: We will survive on the market without expertise. Management never thinks about this.

And also, these people in Puram, they are very pushy. They don't seem to realize that they have much less expertise than we. They are only 25 years old. They think they know everything, but they don't.

It seems that Martin fears becoming superfluous after having transferred his expertise to Puram. To make sense of this development and to still be able to view himself as an established expert, he creates the logical 'Other' for himself: the corresponding perspective of a pushy young Puram engineer. In that sense, every group of other is a creation based on interpretation of one's own situation and not based on objective facts or 'real' cultural difference.

Construction of alternate 'Others' in times of endangerment only takes place as soon and as long as this endangerment is perceived as such. Martin's statement shows that the dominant emic perspective of 'global engineering' still exists: he speaks about 'bad management'. From his perspective, technical expertise lies at the heart of corporate success – not management strategy and techniques. It is thus very likely that the dominant emic discourse of 'we are all engineers' will take over as soon as endangerment is perceived as being non-existent.

Therefore, Martin's contextual discourse of defence also depends on counter-strategies of other actors, in this case on the strategy chosen by young Puram engineers such as Karthik: Karthik does have the power to make Martin 'come back to normal', he can do so through his own contextual strategy of appeasement.

What will happen if Martin and Karthik are united as engineers in such a way? If something goes wrong, that is, corporate crisis occurs, they are likely to blame management 'Others' and not the global community of engineers.

IMPLICATIONS FOR CROSS-CULTURAL MANAGEMENT

As the previous pages have shown for the case of ChipTech, discourses of identity in organizations occur on different levels and largely depend on context and individual agenda. This means: there is no simple explanation to how collective sense is established under changing boundary conditions. Taking an interpretative approach to organizational complexity seems thus the only viable means to study discourses of 'We' and the 'Other' for each setting and not to generalize them. In any complex professional setting, the key question is: when will dormant collective identities become salient? Only if this context is known, cross-cultural management from the emic perspective is possible.

Herein lies the danger of organizational dynamics for the field of cross-cultural management. If employees have the power of reinterpretation and sense-making within a complex organizational field, they might take whatever knowledge they acquire and use it for their own defence. Hence, they might even use intercultural dimensions that are introduced to them in intercultural training. If such a training activity is based on monolithic, static and national-culturally comparative theories, the emic outcome is unclear. If cross-cultural managers in the field are not aware of this new sense that employees might give to their messages, they might thus even fuel potential conflict between sites.

Further research yet has to clarify these uncertainties in detail. However, what seems clear already is the fact that organizational actors make their own sense of change and the Other. This sense is deeply rooted within the organization and consists of a complex agglomeration of categorizations in times of stability and crisis.

The meaning of this conclusion is double-fold: first, actors in the field chose these discourses depending on issues of hierarchy, power, crisis and endangerment. Second, only if cross-cultural managers are aware of these facts can they devise intercultural measures that work at the 'real' intercultural border from the actors' perspective.

RECOMMENDATION TO PRACTITIONERS

Naturally, uncovering emic discourses cannot be a streamlined process. Yet as a checklist, the following questions to the actors should be answered from their perspective:

1. What is considered to be 'good work practice'? What are the requirements and constraints of 'good work practice' of such a kind? This question will deliver dominant emic collective identities, for example, engineers versus management.

2. Who is the respective collective 'Other' in times of stability and in times of change or crisis? What is considered to be a crisis that calls for strategies of defence against actors of other sites? This question will deliver the specific boundary conditions in which dormant emic discourses will become salient. In technical companies that are in the process of knowledge transfer across sites, crisis refers to the fear of losing one's job after having completed knowledge transfer. This fear increases the likelihood that offshore site engineers or management (to be blamed for crisis) are made alien. However, this categorization, too, does not always take place – depending on the counter-strategies of appeasement chosen by the offshore site.

3. What is the impact of the discourse of national cultural difference from the actors' perspective? If they contradict this discourse: when and why are they doing so? This question will deliver the interpretation of etic discourses by the actors in the field and show potential viable cross-cultural management strategies. In technical companies, this means: affirmation of global engineering identity by HR management will most likely increase engineers' motivation to receive intercultural training and learn about potential national cultural differences. Stating the importance of national cultural difference will make HR management themselves be perceived as alien by engineers and decrease engineers' motivation to take national cultural differences into account.

4. What are the 'worst-case combinations' of the above-mentioned boundary conditions? This question will deliver the strongest scenario of conflict based on collective identities. In technical companies this might be the combination of HR management stressing national cultural differences and engineers feeling endangered while transferring knowledge. Under such a scenario, engineers might use learned dimensions of national cultural difference (even though they don't believe in them) to prove that working together with the offshore site cannot work and to overcome their own endangerment.

REFERENCES

Bennett, M. (1986), 'A developmental approach to training for intercultural sensitivity', *International Journal of Intercultural Relations*, **10** (2), 179–95.
Dahlén, T. (1997), *Among the Interculturalists – An Emergent Profession and its Packaging of Knowledge*, Stockholm: Gotab.

Geertz, C. (1973), *The Interpretation of Cultures*, New York: Basic Books.
Goffman, E. (1959), *The Presentation of Self in Everyday Life*, New York: Doubleday.
Gupta, A. and J. Ferguson (eds) (1997), *Anthropological Locations – Boundaries and Grounds of a Field Science*, Berkeley, CA: University of California Press.
Hofstede, G. (1980), *Culture's Consequences: International Differences in Work Related Values*, Beverly Hills, CA: Sage.
Hofstede, G. (2003), *Culture's Consequences: Comparing Values, Behaviors, Institutions and Organizations Across Nations*, London, Thousand Oaks, CA and New Dehli: Sage.
Kunda, G. (1992), *Engineering Culture – Control and Commitment in a High-tech-Cooperation*, Philadelphia, PA: Temple University Press.
Mahadevan, J. (2009), 'Redefining organizational cultures: an interpretative anthropological approach to corporate narratives', *Forum: Qualitative Social Research,* **10**(1), Art. 44, accessed 29 August 2010 at http://nbn-resolving.de/urn:nbn:de:0114-fqs0901440.
Ricoeur, P. (1992), *Oneself as Another*, Chicago, IL: University of Chicago Press.
Trompenaars, F. and C. Hampden-Turner (1997), *Riding the Waves of Culture: Understanding Cultural Diversity in Global Business*, London: Nicholas Brealey.

9. Negotiating meaning across borders (finally!): Western management training in Eastern Europe

Snejina Michailova and Graham Hollinshead

INTRODUCTION

In this chapter we examine evolution in the design and development of Western management training initiatives in Bulgaria over a period of over a decade. A starting proposition for our analysis is that the orchestrated flow of management knowledge from West to East, instigated by prominent Western agencies, has occurred in a fashion that has been insensitive to the existing stock of knowledge and precise training needs of indigenous (local) participants. Indeed, as a concomitant of the precipitous flow of financial assistance into the East European (EE) region, we argue that the flow of knowledge 'aid' has been predicated on underlying precepts of the benefits of 'shock therapy' and carried with it the exhortation for rapid and perhaps unachievable managerial and organizational change.

AID PROGRAMMES IN EASTERN EUROPE

There has been recognition over the period of reform that EE countries have sorely needed outside help (Benson and Clay, 1992). In the wake of the revolutions in 1989, the Group of 24 industrialized countries embarked on aid programmes in Hungary and in Poland with the European Union (EU) taking the major role (Turnock, 1997). Initially, aid was offered in return for the acceptance of five basic values: the rule of law, respect for human rights, free elections, political pluralism and progress towards a market economy (Pelkmans and Murphy, 1991). Technical assistance to promote trade was fostered by the programme of Pologne-Hongrie Actions pour la Reconversion Economique (PHARE) which prioritized the following areas: food aid and the restructuring of Polish agriculture; improved access for Hungarian and Polish goods in Western markets, European Bank for Reconstruction and Development investment in energy, industry and services: environmental improvement and improved environmental and vocational training for students and managers, particularly in financial and banking services. Although the programme was initially directed exclusively towards Poland and Hungary, it was extended to all EE countries in 1991. PHARE has allocated about 4 billion euros from 1990 to 1994, this being increased to close to 7 billion euros for the period 1995 to 1999. In recent years the focus of efforts has shifted to embrace support for legislative frameworks and administrative structures, the promotion of democracy and civil society and for investment in infrastructure, including cross-border cooperation.

We should note that since the earliest stages of reform, EE countries have been the recipients of various assistance packages from the West, with financial and technical/vocational initiatives frequently running in parallel. Over the period of reform international organizations, such as the International Monetary Fund (IMF), the World Bank and the London Club of creditor nations, have played a role in shaping the 'new European' economies and became key factors in generating EE business cycles. Indeed, structural and cultural reforms in Eastern Europe were accompanied by powerful international exhortation, with financial strings attached, to radicalize moves towards market liberalism. If the extension of financial aid carried with it the obligation for the transitional economies to demonstrate capitalist performativity in the short, rather than the medium to long term, then it is understandable that the injection of new management ideas and techniques to fill post-socialist organizational deficits would scarcely constitute an act of international altruism.

It makes sense to examine Western management training in Eastern Europe within the wider spectrum of unfolding political, economic and social eventualities outlined above. Although it may be tempting to attribute ideological and professional neutrality to international trainers and the programmes they initiate and deliver, it is our contention that the circumstances of power disparity between the early post-socialist EE transitional economies to which the programmes were targeted, and the Western developed nations from which they originated, profoundly conditioned the content as well as the social and pedagogic orientation of such programmes. In seeking to deconstruct the phenomenological purpose and meaning of PHARE (and similar) programmes, it is important to trace their origins as manifestations of Western 'assistance' to the post-socialist countries as part of a grand scale quid pro quo in which tangible moves towards democratization and market liberalism needed to be demonstrated within the former socialist bloc in Europe. Our observations, arguments and analysis are based on our theoretical interest in the issue and our intensive involvement in Western management training programs conducted in Eastern Europe over a period of 15 years.

STRUCTURE OF THE CHAPTER

After presenting the empirical inspiration of our analysis, which documents strategic developments in two sequential PHARE-sponsored knowledge transfer programmes from 1992 to 2003, we reflect upon the central transitional tendencies inherent in these programmes which have reflected socio-political and economic growth in the host locality. Notably, we focus on (1) the devolution of responsibility for programme design and delivery to local providers and experts and (2) the modification of training content from a Western conceived notion of pre-packaged knowledge supply from West to East, existing at a high level of abstraction, to a more negotiated form of concrete knowledge creation with specific reference to the problems and experiences of Bulgarian management 'clientele'. In seeking to make sense of these developments we draw upon influential contributions from the field of knowledge creation and transfer (Lillrank, 1995). Our central argument is that, in order to be meaningful, international forms of knowledge transfer and learning should ideally be iterative in nature, reflecting growing maturity in the experience and status of *both* trainers and learners.

We do not wish to engage in a critique of new business narratives per se, but rather to consider how emerging normative typologies in the West present a template for reform in both West and Eastern Europe. In considering Western training programmes to assist reform in Eastern Europe we imply that trainers were (and may still be) drawn into untested propositions that organizational problems in Eastern Europe merely constitute more extreme versions of familiar Western malaises and thus are amenable to a similar set of prescriptions for their resolution. The following quotation from a Western trainer engaged in the earlier stages of a PHARE programme in Bulgaria illustrates this position well: 'I didn't have any special thoughts about the fact that I should teach in Bulgaria. It was about passing on as much of *our* [emphasis added] knowledge as possible in a way that was understandable for them. This was actually my starting point.' As normative knowledge transfer has formed the basis for much Western training and developmental activity in Eastern Europe, particularly in the 1990s, it is instructive at this stage to distinguish it from processes of a different nature, namely negotiating meaning in the process of exchanging and co-creating knowledge among parties that have for a long time belonged to and identified with different regimes and ways of society organization.

TWO SEQUENTIAL CASES IN WEST-EAST MANAGEMENT KNOWLEDGE TRANSFER

The cases forming the empirical basis for this chapter may be regarded as major international development projects funded substantially by the EU or

Western governmental sources. Bulgaria Training 1 (BT1) and Bulgaria Training 2 (BT2) are the disguised names of two sequential projects instigated from 1992 to 1996 and 2000 to 2003, respectively. Primary empirical data of two kinds were collected from 1990 to 2003. The first source was the body of documentation and written materials to which we had almost unlimited access as a result of the involvement of one of us in both projects. These included terms of reference, applications for funding, module descriptions, reports, evaluations, letters, e-mail messages, minutes of meetings and the like. Second, as one of us was closely involved in the teaching and management of both programmes (for example, participating in designing and negotiating content and delivery, writing case studies and 'delivering' training), we also employed participant observation to collect data in the naturally occurring contexts of the phenomena we were interested in (Miles and Huberman, 1994) and to investigate events and encounters that involved interactions and inter-pretations (Waddington, 1994). Examining West-East management training over a 12-year period implied that we could attribute meaning and causality to a sequence of events that we would not be able to recognize if we witnessed them as 'snapshots'. Similarly, motives of major project stakeholders became more discernible as they were woven into a series of interconnected and sequential actions, and reviewed and revisited post hoc (Michailova and Hollinshead, 2009).

BT1

The PHARE projects in Bulgaria were delivered under the auspices of the EU Restructuring, Privatization and Development Program. BT1 was offered over a four-year period in two phases, from 1992 to 1994 and from 1994 to 1996, drawing trainers from various Western European Business Schools. The espoused training philosophy underlying BT1 is captured in the following quotation from the stated terms of reference of the PHARE project in Bulgaria:

> Our educational approach will emphasize the development of personal skills and attitudes, including creativity, conscious acceptance and management of risks, together with the capacity of developing a global vision that can shape future busi-ness evolution. Furthermore, it will have the specificity of balancing these overall capabilities with the particular abilities for effective implementation within Bulgarian enterprises and economic institutions. The educational philosophy behind our proposed training approach could best be described as 'interactive'. Teaching methods will employ a multitude of teaching tools such as case studies and case discussions, class assignments and class discussions, business games and field projects, along with traditional lectures which will be designed along a specific phased structure ... The exercise will assist students in applying tools to specific problems, in learning how to work effectively in teams and under pressure, and in

preparing effective solutions and presentations of their decisions. (Technical and financial proposal for two-year contract, July 1994)

Despite the interactive intent of the programme designers, its prescriptive and explicitly Westernized framing of business concepts and philosophy was evidenced through the content of all course modules. Courses of up to six days were provided, the number of participants varying between 20 and 35. Target groups for BT1 constituted state-owned enterprises undergoing restructuring, small and medium-sized enterprises, ministries and central and local government agencies and municipalities involved in the privatization process (Hollinshead and Michailova, 2001). Managers from various organizational levels constituted the clientele for the programme. The predominant pedagogic device for knowledge transfer was classroom-based training and learning in a number of major Bulgarian cities (Hollinshead and Michailova, 2001). While company-based project work and in-house training sessions had been envisaged in terms of reference, in practice these approaches rarely materialized. Nineteen different courses were delivered in English with simultaneous translation into Bulgarian. Teaching materials (copies of articles, book chapters, transparencies and so on) were made available in English and Bulgarian languages. Over the period of operation of BT1 and BT2 a process of 'continuous improvement' guided the deliberations of programme designers. A critical point of concern at an early stage was the all-embracing nature of client selection, including 'old' as well as 'new' style managers and administrators.

BT2

Following an internal bidding process, phase two of the program was delivered by a larger consortium of Western business schools. While some refinements occurred in programme content, in general no major modifications occurred. The client group focus was switched from state-owned to mainly private and small and medium-sized enterprises. Also, greater homogeneity was achieved among participants in terms of age and work background, this rendering a more 'switched on' managerial grouping in the classroom, and promoting consonance in teaching and learning agendas.

BT2 was also sponsored by PHARE and organized and led, at least in its early stages, by major consortium partners responsible for BT1. However BT2 manifested important differences in design and delivery. In particular, the Bulgarian branch of a large international consultancy company was a consortium member alongside the three Western academic institutions. BT2 comprised two major elements: (1) enterprise-based management development aiming to improve management practices evident in Bulgarian companies and (2) management training and consultancy services for Bulgarian business aiming at upgrading the country's business training and consulting sector (Michailova and Hollinshead, 2009). Accordingly, while BT1 had relied solely on classroom-based teaching, BT2 was designed to focus on problem-centred actions in Bulgarian companies, with Western experts being expected to solve concrete problems with Bulgarian managers in the field. In keeping with a transitioning, and more grounded, philosophy of management knowledge transfer over the period of operation of BT1 and BT2, several critical points of systemic reorientation were evidenced. Among those were the involvement of local experts in the design of programmes, narrowing down the indigenous (Bulgarian) client base from a broad cross-section of the managerial population to one which possesses the 'correct' credentials in terms of factors such as age (less than 44) and English language ability, and training delivery in English in order to facilitate extended and free dialogue and the sharing of ideas.

KNOWLEDGE FLOWS IN WESTERN-EE MANAGEMENT TRAINING PROGRAMMES: A MODEL

Investigating the transfer of management innovations from Japan to the West Lillrank (1995) formulated a model capturing the complexity of knowledge

	Multi-purpose concepts; Limited reflection	Academic knowledge; Theoretical interpretations
High abstraction of knowledge	*Co-created knowledge based on negotiated meanings*	*Exchange of situated knowledge*
Low abstraction of knowledge	Solutions to practical problems; Quick fixes of urgent issues *Transporting knowledge without concerns regarding contextualization*	(Western) case descriptions; De-contextualized application *Knowledge pre-packaged with meaning*
	Knowledge driven by East European participants' needs	Knowledge driven by Western trainers

Figure 9.1   Knowledge flows in Western-EE management training programmes

flows along two dimensions, namely the level of abstraction of knowledge and the key driver of the knowledge flows. We utilize the model to provide insight into the multiple knowledge flows taking place in Western management training programs in Eastern Europe. Figure 9.1 illustrates the model, the italicized additions pointing towards our modifications.

In essence, the notion of abstraction refers not only to the complexity of the idea or system to be transferred, but also to the number and types of social interfaces involved in the travelling of ideas across borders. A clear implication is that institutional, cultural, ideological, psychic and other kinds of distance between the actors involved in the knowledge flows will heighten its level of abstraction. Demand and supply in Figure 9.1 refers to the approach adopted by the actors in the knowledge flows, with demand-driven approaches focusing on the provision of solutions to specific problems and supply-driven approaches concentrating upon formulating questions, building understanding and developing theoretical capability.

HOW KNOWLEDGE FLOWS CHANGED AS TRANSITION PROGRESSED

Numerous Western management training programmes in Eastern Europe in the early stage of transitions would be located in the upper right hand quadrant of Lillrank's (1995) model. These programmes tended to be unequivocally supply-driven and typically exclusively designed and delivered by the agents of Western academic consortia. Programme content was usually characterized by a high level of abstraction, curricula adhering closely to orthodox academic fare in Western business schools, comprising functional subjects, such as corporate strategy, financial management, marketing, human resource management and the like. Over time, signs of a gradual shift towards demand orientation became evident, particularly as 'the client base' became skewed in favour of private, rather than state sector, management. There was also some evidence of growing usage of lower abstraction teaching materials, and particularly local(ized) case studies. Some of these teaching mechanisms, however, tended to be regarded as facile and superfluous by an audience that had grown used to a transmission-belt of knowledge delivery (Hollinshead and Michailova, 2001).

Drawing on Lillrank (1995), the sudden infusion of highly abstracted Western managerial knowledge into post-reform Eastern Europe resembled the flow of high voltage electricity into a distant circuit inadequately equipped to reduce the current to a usable level. As a corollary of the effects of shock therapy associated with financial assistance, the injection of unrefined and idealized managerial prescription into this post-socialist territory occurred in a fashion incompatible with the prevailing status and nature of existing knowledge, organizational experience and learning.

The following quotation from a representative of a Western consulting company based in Bulgaria attending BT1 serves to poignantly illustrate the above proposition:

> There were only a few links with Bulgarian reality, but I don't think that this can be expected from Western teachers. First of all, they know nothing about Bulgarian practice and, secondly, Bulgaria is a peculiar country that is stuck in its transition between socialism and capitalism. Our economy does not provide typical examples to illustrate Western theories. It would be much better if the teachers knew a little about Bulgaria. The lack of this type of knowledge made the training difficult, especially for people who were not able to speak English or who were not economists.

In the context of the broader attempts to re-engineer the EE economies along liberal capitalist lines through international financial aid, the 'clientele' may have been forgiven for perceiving episodes in the classroom as auxiliary propagandist exercises to persuade them that existing skills, attributes and values possessed little or no functional value in the new era. Indeed, if the travesty of financial aid packages from the West was its overbearing transcendence of existing institutional arrangements, the travesty associated with international knowledge transfer was that it failed to acknowledge and nurture the status of indigenous knowledge, including tacit knowledge that tends to be high context in nature (Hall and Hall, 1987) and that consists of deeply ingrained cognitive models, beliefs and perceptions. Putting knowledge in context (understood not as a static set of surrounding conditions, but rather a dynamic process of which individual cognition is only a part) is important because knowledge-creating processes are essentially context-specific in terms of who participates and how they participate in the process.

If we hypothesize that a gradualist approach to assistance efforts in the field of management learning had occurred at the outset, then possibilities would undoubtedly have emerged for incorporating indigenous knowledge into new domains of knowledge creation and co-creation. Again following Lillrank (1995) and the model illustrated in Figure 9.1, it is likely that low abstraction channels are most appropriate at early stages of transfer, without the need for deep reflection and when EE managers were in urgent need of management 'quick fixes' at an early stage of transformation. However, it is then through the application of demand-driven approaches, conditioned by tacit knowledge, that the value of the new principle or practice can be realized. More generally, we should note that drawing upon tacit knowledge is necessary to reap the benefits of experiential learning (Kolb, 1984) and double-loop learning (Argyris and Schön, 1978), the virtues of which were denied to Bulgarian recipients of 'shock therapy' knowledge aid.

Whilst the overriding needs of EE managers, particularly in the early stages of reform, were for quick solutions to pressing problems, the major strategic thrust of training assistance from the West was the front-end loaded delivery of idealized Western business orthodoxy in an unrefined fashion, jolting the consciousness of indigenous audiences unsympathetically towards market orientation. The provision of management knowledge assistance on this basis, whilst being consistent with grander scale efforts of powerful international bodies, and particularly the IMF, to gain rapid conversion to liberal market principles in transitional economies, can ultimately be measured only by its wastefulness. Holden (2002, p. 83), for example, refers to the 'mammoth crusade if enlightenment' in the post-socialist countries as 'non productive and therefore a waste of money'.

It should be pointed out, however, that wasted resources of knowledge in bolstering the process of transformation are not only at the expense of the Western providers, but also of the EE participants whose potentially invaluable tacit, localized insights were largely laid waste. As Lillrank (1995) has implied, a more benign and productive spiral of knowledge creation can occur through the assisted metamorphosis of prosaic into more sophisticated and theorized knowledge forms over time. This is what we refer to as continuous negotiating of meaning in the knowledge flows across borders. This lesson, following Kolb (1984) and other authorities, of gradually building experiential knowledge into more highly abstracted forms, provides the theoretical antithesis for the reality of international training assistance over the period of reform. The belated devolution of responsibility for management development activity to local providers may now be suggestive of a Western commitment to embrace indigenous knowledge resources in a more productive fashion, although for doubters of the fundamentalist power of 'the market' to be satisfied, this initiative will need to be rapidly extended beyond the ranks of selected proselytes.

IMPLICATIONS FOR PRACTICE AND RECOMMENDATIONS

This chapter concurs with the critical voices that have been heard in the recent literature on Western management training and education in Eastern Europe. We have built up our main arguments by making use of key notions such as evolution of training programmes, travesty of assistance and negotiated meaning in order to understand and illuminate key features of the nature of knowledge diffused as well as of the learning processes in these programmes. It is important not to invalidate social and management experiences and well-established traditions of knowledge diffusion in Eastern Europe that have been existing prior to the start of booming Western management training interventions in the region. Instead, we emphasize the significance of continuous, never-ending learning that relates to the growing maturity of both EE managers and Western trainers.

In drawing lessons for practitioners from our study, which we would tentatively suggest may have relevance beyond the immediate domain of 'set piece' international training and development initiatives to the broader fields of international collaboration in joint ventures, strategic alliances and the like, we would suggest that it is incumbent on training providers to reaffirm the principles of 'embedded learning' beyond their own national borders (Michailova and Hollinshead, 2009). Experiential learning, which encourages subjects to embark upon an 'inward journey' of thinking, analysis and conceptualization, possesses considerable validity in transitional economies where management actors strive to make sense of, and react to, environmental uncertainty and change.

In purely practical terms, in light of the foregoing analysis, those formulating international training programmes may well be advised to (1) actively involve training recipients in the design of training programmes; (2) involve local (and international) experts in the delivery of training; (3) formulate training materials so that they have relevance to the socio-political and economic distinctiveness of the host environment as well as injecting international perspectives; and (4) foster a collegiate atmosphere for the sharing of knowledge amongst local and international training participants and providers and encourage the creation of new, and negotiated, knowledge and meaning. In summary, if the knowledge of experts is to be meaningful in emergent international forms and configurations, it is likely to have to be 'given away'!

REFERENCES

Argyris, C. and D.A. Schön (1978), *Organizational Learning: A Theory of Action Perspective,* Reading, MA: Addison-Wesley.

Benson, C. and E.J. Clay (1992), 'Eastern Europe and the former Soviet Union: economic change, social welfare and aid', in *ODI Special Report,* London: Overseas Development Institute.

Hall, E.T. and M. Reed Hall (1987), *Hidden Differences: Doing Business with the Japanese,* Garden City, NY: Doubleday.

Holden, N.J. (2002), *Cross-Cultural Management: A Knowledge Management Perspective,* Harlow: FT Prentice Hall.

Hollinshead, G. and S. Michailova (2001), 'Blockbusters or bridge-builders? The role of western trainers in developing new entrepreneuralism in Eastern Europe', *Management Learning,* **32**(4), 419–36.

Kolb, D.A. (1984), *Experiential Learning: Experience as the Source of Learning and Development,* Englewood Cliffs, NJ: Prentice Hall.

Lillrank, P. (1995), 'The transfer of management innovations from Japan', *Organization Studies*, **16**(6), 971–89.

Michailova, S. and G. Hollinshead (2009), 'Western management training in Eastern Europe: trends and developments over a decade', *Human Resource Development International*, **12**(2), 117–33.

Miles, M.B. and M. Huberman (1994), *Qualitative Data Analysis: An Extended Sourcebook*, 2nd edn, Thousand Oaks, CA: Sage.

Pelkmans, J. and A. Murphy (1991), 'Catapulted into leadership: the community's trade and aid policies vis-a-vis Eastern Europe', *Journal of European Integration*, **14**, 125–51.

Turnock, D. (1997), *The East European Economy in Context: Communism and the Transition (Eastern Europe Since 1945)*, London: Routledge.

Waddington, D. (1994), 'Participant observation', in C. Cassell and G. Symon (eds), *Qualitative Methods in Organizational Research: A Practical Guide*, London: Sage, pp. 107–22.

10. Intercultural integration in Sino–Brazilian joint ventures

Guilherme Azevedo[1]

性相近 習相遠

Men's natures are alike, it is their habits that carry them far apart.

(Mencius in *'The Three Character Classic'*)

THE INTEGRATION DINNER

A friend of mine once told me a story. He had spent two years in Sweden studying mechanical engineering. There was a clear separation between the Swedes and the international students. The two groups lived in different places and, according to him, the Swedes did not hang out or mix much with the international students. There had been a polite relationship within the classrooms but a very low overall social interaction.

The courses were in English, already a second language for most of the foreign students, and they had not made much effort to learn Swedish. During the holidays the Swedes would go home and the foreigners would stay at the university or travel in Europe. Most of the foreigners, as told my friend, had never been invited to a Swedish house or spent time with a Swedish family.

The foreign students gradually started stereotyping their local colleagues as being distant, never doing anything on impulse and caring just about their own business. (I do not know what the Swedes thought of the international students.) After a year and half – with graduation approaching – the administrators of the programme decided to take action and organized an integration dinner. But things did not go as planned.

Arriving at the large dining table, the international students flocked to one part of the table and the Swedes to the other. As the dinner started each side group engaged in a separate conversation. After a while, perhaps being uncomfortable with the lack of integration in their integration dinner and encouraged by the wine, a local student tried to start a conversation with a foreigner colleague. He interrupted a nearby Italian with a friendly question:

'So, why did you decide to come to Sweden?' The Italian stopped gesticulating and talking for a second, turned to him, quipped: 'Because of the weather', turned back to his side of the table and continued his conversation.

It was too late to start the integration.

I asked my friend if his colleague's reaction was not too rude. He reflected for a moment before answering: 'In retrospect, I think it was. But, at the time, I found it just right and very funny. We did not care about integration anymore.'

The end of the story is anticlimactic: the Swedes and foreigners finished their course and continued their lives. Perhaps they missed the opportunity of experiencing a richer intercultural exchange and forming a larger international network, but they got their degrees and, at the end, nobody got hurt.

Organizations however are unlikely to perform well if composed of groups unable to collaborate productively. In this case, a better cultural integration certainly is needed.

STUDYING INTEGRATION IN MULTICULTURAL ORGANIZATIONS

Typical examples of multicultural organizations (that is, whose workforce comes from different cultures) are multinational subsidiaries abroad, international joint ventures and international mergers and acquisitions. The academic literature is replete with examples of such organizations struggling with cultural integration and conflicts.

Interestingly, these texts (for example, Byun and Ybema, 2005; Pardi, 2005) very often repeat the plot depicted in the integration dinner: different cultural groups are put together; poor preparation, inadequate structure and contextual factors conspire to make the integration difficult; a series of micro-dynamics prevents integration and increases the separation; negative stereotypes are developed as indifference mounts to cultural conflict; and, one day, people realize that it seems too late or too costly to pursue the cultural integration that would allow a fruitful collaboration. This is a trap to be avoided.

In this chapter I tackle the problem of how to integrate different cultures within an organization. My investigation is based upon the direct observation of managers and workers that are 'out there', facing the issue of intercultural integration. This approach reflects Schein's (1996, p. 239) belief that 'organization studies will not mature as a field until we spend much more time in observing and absorbing these other [organizational] cultures [and in] learning to see them from the insider's perspective …'

THE CASE OF SINO–BRAZILIAN JOINT VENTURES

Looking for cases of combinations of culturally and geographically distant organizations, I became interested in the Brazilian joint ventures in China.

China and Brazil are almost at antipodes. If you could dig a hole in a Rio de Janeiro beach to get to the exact other side of the planet, you would miss China by just seven degrees. Moreover, they also appear to be at 'cultural antipodes'. There has been virtually no historical relation between China and Brazil, and their national cultures are defined by unrelated or opposed traditions: Sino-Tibetan versus Latin-Romance language families; Confucianism, Taoism and Buddhism versus Catholicism and Afro-American religions; Eastern millenary civilization versus Western new-world immigration land; single-party socialism versus multiparty capitalism and so on.

China and Brazil are very far apart and we should therefore expect a lot of difficulties – or plenty of spectacular cultural collisions (Hamada, 1991, p. 5) – when Chinese and Brazilians try to work together.

I embarked to China with this prospect in mind. But, surprisingly, the Sino-Brazilian organizations I studied there were not particularly marked by cultural conflict.

I gathered the data through participant observation and interviews in China in June and July of 2006. I studied two Sino-Brazilian joint ventures, one with 12 years in China and another with four, and I collected some additional data during visits to a division of a US-Chinese joint venture managed by Brazilian expatriates and to a trade office representing a Brazilian company in China.[2]

This data collection, although too short in traditional ethnographic practice, followed the principles of ethnography applied to organizations (for example, Brannen, 1996; Schwartzman, 1993) and took place within the organizations and at external spaces, including employees clubs, homes, hotel lobbies, restaurants, parks and even a traditional Chinese bath.

INTERCULTURAL INTEGRATION

Tolstoy opens his *Anna Karenina* with the line: 'Happy families are all alike; every unhappy family is unhappy in its own way.' Similarly, in organizations, there are many more ways to fail than to succeed.

Particularly, one path to failure for multicultural organizations is the inability of developing a minimal level of internal intercultural integration. This common ground – or the path leading to this construction – gives better survival and success chances to multicultural organizations.

Based on my observations, and to state it clearly, the overall argument of this chapter is: given a minimal set of preconditions, 'a discourse of proximity' combined with 'practices of micro-integration' leads to the emergence of 'intercultural integration'.

Figure 10.1 Intercultural integration

The 'construction of a sense of proximity' happens through the diffusion of a body of arguments indicating that the different groups are culturally close to each other. 'Micro-dynamics of integration' are collections of practices and social norms that emerge within and around the organization to support an overarching integration. This simultaneous development of discourse and action allows the collaboration needed to reach positive tangible results (productivity, quality, innovation and so on).

The antithesis of this equation is the trap to be avoided: the construction of 'discourses of difference' that feed 'micro-dynamics of separation' and jeopardize any potential collaboration.

CONSTRUCTION OF A SENSE OF PROXIMITY

I call 'sense of proximity' a certain set of discourses that, during my field-work, Brazilians and Chinese have put together to argue that they are closer to each other than one might usually expect. Their arguments referred mainly to individuals (the proximity and similarities between Chinese and Brazilians) and to nationalities (the proximity and similarities between China and Brazil).

Because we know Brazilians and Chinese are very different, the sense of proximity is collectively constructed as a partial selection of some objective similarities and by the approximate adaptation, exaggeration or invention of others.

At the national level, for instance, they indicated this proximity by arguing that both countries share the same level of development:

> We are countries that are similar in development. It helps us to be together. We may have a feeling of being much from the same country.[3] (Chinese manager)

The Chinese treat you well. It is different than being in the US or in Europe. You are not going to feel discriminated by a Chinese because you are a 'cucaracha'.[4] (Brazilian director)

At the individual level, the sense of proximity is built as they unveil and emphasize similarities in behavior and values:

The Chinese is, by character, very generous to those who are visiting him ... This also makes them similar to Brazilians. In my view, the Chinese is the Brazilian of Asia. We have a lot in common: the talkativeness, the noise, the sense of humor. (Brazilian director)

We [Chinese and Brazilians] have many things in common. We have football, we are friendly, humorous, and like jokes. We are also very diligent. We work hard and seriously. We know how to make jokes and work well too. (Chinese manager)

As they point to these similarities, they draw generalizations based on their shared personal experiences. The relative cultural proximity is also communicated by 'out-grouping' other nationalities (that is, by indicating that they are closer to each other when compared with other nationalities):

I even think that we are closer to the Chinese than we are to some Europeans, as it could be the case of Germans or Englishmen. (Brazilian director)

Working with Brazilians is easier than working with North Americans, French or even people from Singapore. It's amazing because [Singaporeans] have the same cultural roots than we have. But with Brazilians it's easier because we treat each other as being at the same level ... It may be more important than having the same cultural root or speaking the same language. (Chinese general-director)

This is therefore more than just a sense of closeness based on cultural proximity. In some cases, the absence of previous cultural contact can also be an asset:

I had no idea about Brazil before; just TV and newspaper showing big festival and music. I saw information on internet [and I saw] a lot of different people in Brazil. (Chinese supervisor)

In general they don't know much about Brazil ... If you are American or European there may be more restriction. If you are Japanese it is even worse. This is because of their history and the Japanese occupation during the war. (Brazilian supervisor)

The absence of a negative stereotype is already a good start. In particular, Brazilians in China have the advantage of not being associated with countries that, during the late nineteenth and early twentieth centuries, extended their imperial ambitions over China.

For me, deep in the mind of Chinese people, there is always this feeling of China being vulnerable and underdeveloped. Maybe the relation toward Brazilians is facilitated because of this. (Chinese general-director)

It is not openly said, [but] the Chinese ... tend to dislike the Western nations that in history tried to occupy and exploit China. (Brazilian director)

Obviously, not all international joint ventures may count with this advantage. If a negative image already exists, managers should do their best to not let a bad geopolitical past, history or pre-existent stereotype play against the integration. The sooner the tendency is reversed the better, please remember the integration dinner.

MICRO-DYNAMICS OF INTEGRATION

The circulation of discourses of proximity allowed a close coexistence where real practices of integration could flourish. As we start to observe these practices (that is, the other side of the construction of a sense of proximity), we enter the territory of the various micro-dynamics of integration.

Within the organizations, the close coexistence has been encouraged and, sometimes, created by design. An example is a company policy that has made all departments deliberately mix:

In the daily work there is really no difference because of nationality. The departments are mixed. That is very important. And both parts work very well together, compared to other programs I saw, really very well. We had no real hard time because of conflict. (Chinese director)

Practices of integration also developed beyond the organizational gates. As the joint ventures started, many Chinese played the roles of hosts or guides to the Brazilians who, in turn, tried to match this generosity. The Chinese would assist the Brazilians and their families in shopping, finding leisure activities and solving a number of day-to-day problems. They would invite each other to community and family celebrations setting a regime of reciprocity that also allowed a better understanding of the other's culture.

This also created the opportunity for the Brazilians to try to live beyond the Western ghettoes we sometimes see in larger Chinese cities. A Brazilian who had lived in China for more than ten years explained to me:

People should go out there and be exposed to see what China is really about ... There is the guy who lives within what I call the 'embassies ghetto' ... He may be in China for four or five years and won't see a thing. The same is true about the companies. The guy comes as an expatriate to work for, let's say, Volkswagen. He does not even like the Germans that much. But he works with Germans. And his neighbor is a German. And at night he goes with the family to have beer with the Germans. F***, if it was about living with the Germans he should go to Germany, not to China! (Brazilian director)

Activities beyond working hours helped reinforce the connection within the working environment. Most typically, people told me about the importance of eating, drinking (and even smoking) together to create strong bonds.

Another fine example of integration outside of work, which has occurred in both joint ventures, has been the creation of soccer teams just for fun or to play in tournaments involving other companies:

After we put together the team the integration improved a lot. The Chinese really like it ... They are playful but also take it very seriously ... they 'give their blood' when playing against other factories. Soccer became an important thing here. (Brazilian manager)

Playing together, they have reinforced a close coexistence inside and outside the organizations. Indeed, playing and joking have became central to allow Brazilians and Chinese to learn how to interact in a new cultural setting.

I have also observed that the progressive construction of an intercultural integration resembles a new acculturation. Children observe and play to, one could say, 'learn' a first culture; and the freedom of playing also help adults to 'learn' a second culture. I comment on three particular aspects of such 're-acculturation'.

Reserving Judgement and Showing Respect for Others' Culture

A fundamental basis to sustain the intercultural integration is to respect the other culture, show respect and recognize the differences:

You see people smiling and respecting other culture background. It is very important. (Chinese manager)

You need to adapt. It is as hard for them as it is for us. We need respect and humbleness from both sides. (Brazilian manager)

As a micro-dynamic of integration, this positive attitude towards the other complements the construction of a discourse of proximity that never denies the existence of real cultural differences. Proximity perhaps, but they have never expected the other part to fully understand their culture. Recognizing this limitation is important because it grants the other an intercultural slack that facilitates the integration:

I don't think that a foreigner would understand [our culture] ... The Brazilians are not Chinese so we cannot have the same requirements. Here we respect and accept the differences on both sides. (Chinese manager)

It would be really difficult to reach a stage where we cease being 'the other'. We may get very close but it is always them and us. (Brazilian director)

Interestingly, they sometimes even developed mechanisms of social control against negative stereotyping or other behaviours that could jeopardize the integration climate:

It all depends on the guy's posture. He may be someone who complains too much. He comes and: 'I don't like this food', 'this thing is dirty' ... Tomorrow he is there again 'this food is not good', 'stuff is not clean'. Nobody can bear a person like this! ... Here people have a good attitude. They don't like this complaining thing. They tell him to stop or even give him some silent treatment. (Brazilian director)

The Cultural Guest Goes the Extra Mile

Both groups had to make concessions. However, in the studied cases, the Brazilians were the cultural minority within the organizations and, even more so, in the Chinese society at large:

We are the minority here. I think that this is very clear ... Since the beginning here in China, we always tried to do the best to respect their way of working and be extremely careful to allow the longevity of the company here. You need to be careful when dealing with a different reality. (Brazilian manager)

The Brazilians accepted to go the extra mile to adapt to the Chinese day-to-day activities. Except for those productive processes and managerial practices consciously transplanted from Brazil, all remained as Chinese as possible. A Brazilian gave me an example of what he called a 'policy of zero-concession': the only changes to the factory facilities have been to some Western model toilets.
Another commonly cited example was food:

The food here is Chinese. We never tried to have it done the Brazilian way ... and I think the Brazilians take it with good humor ... We could perhaps have some black beans or coffee brought from Brazil. But I think nobody ever asked. Many actually started drinking tea as the Chinese do. (Brazilian manager)

This approach nevertheless produced some victims since adapting to the local Chinese food was problematic for some:

Food for me is the problem, man. Now I have a strategy. I wake up a half-hour earlier to have time to a really reinforced breakfast ... I get even some protein supplements ... I think I eat three times more than in Brazil. Then, at lunch time, I just eat a little bit. I almost just pretend I eat. Some days it is ok. But others, ... the smell is already enough to make me sick. I try controlling myself but I know they can read in my face. They see I don't like the food and I feel embarrassed ... The girls who serve are disappointed. But what can I do? ... There is some stuff that I really can't eat. (Brazilian manager)

It shows how important it became to try not to offend the other group's cultural sensibility. Interestingly, some Chinese downplayed such problems and put them in the 'intercultural slack' bag:

If Brazilian person don't like Chinese food. No problem. [There are] different food. I see Brazilian person like or not like. Not need to talk. Look at the face. Different food. In Brazil good food and food I don't like. No problem. (Chinese supervisor)

Overall both groups appreciated the collective effort of reserving judgement and showing respect, as they also appreciated policies to reduce separation. In one of the organizations, both Chinese and Brazilians repeatedly referred to a story that became part of their organizational mythology. Once the Brazilian partner acquired the 50 per cent share that belonged to a European company, they unified the cafeteria and eliminated a number of the benefits exclusive for expatriates, including memberships in social clubs used by foreigners and reserved meeting spaces within the company.

All these micro-dynamics – based on implicit social norms or explicit polices and managerial decisions – contributed to a progressive integration. As time elapsed and new cohorts of expatriates joined in, they also profited from the accumulated effort to build a positive image, which represented a sort of stock of goodwill:

The Brazilian may be more integrative than other Westerns. But it is still very difficult. I think it is perhaps easier for us because of the Brazilians who came before. We profit from the good impression they've left here. (Brazilian manager)

Docking into Others' Cultural Traditions

As Chinese and Brazilians interacted, particular cultural dispositions belonging to one side would eventually be adapted to frame the relationship between them. Here is an example:

In my mind, [some] Chinese saw the Brazilians ... as teachers because [their parent company] had strong experience and technology. And the Brazilians were happy to be the teachers because they appreciated that Chinese want[ed] to learn. You have to understand that in China the relation of teacher and student is very important. It is more like ... [pause] more like the master and the apprentice. (Chinese manager)

They called him professor ... There is something about being loyal to the one that teaches that is very important ... So, when he went back to Brazil, I'm not kidding, there were these two tough guys from the assembling line with tears in their eyes. (Brazilian manager)

A binary construction representing a hierarchical arrangement (as: master–apprentice, parent–son/daughter, older-sibling–younger-sibling, boss–worker, government official–citizen and so on) makes more sense for the Chinese than for the Brazilians. It exemplifies how sometimes the Brazilians got 'docked into' some of the peculiarities of the Chinese culture.

As they progressively understood the other's culture, they also found ways to intervene without trespassing some cultural limits. The importance of protecting face to the Chinese is an example:

A Chinese working in your team is going to do all the possible to not bring you information showing that a colleague of him has made a mistake. They do every-thing to protect a colleague's face. He is going to tell you he doesn't know, he forgot, or even that he lost that paper or file ... by the kind of smile he has in his face you realize that he knows who did it but he is not going to tell you. This is very important to them. So, ... just respect it. Never force them do go against it and they will respect you for that. (Brazilian director)

Moreover, sometimes they consciously used the other's cultural arrange-ment to serve a practical purpose:

Their tendency to communicate so fast among them, this gossip thing, it also helps ... For instance: there is a part that comes from the line with some small problem ..., just a matter of aesthetics. You know who did the job. But you ... have to real-ize that if you talk directly to him the others will be paying attention and the person will be offended. So you just throw a comment in the air. You say it to anyone, ... as if you were passing by and just making a kind of generic observation: – 'hey. So, do you see this part here. It is quite good don't you think? It deserves perhaps just a bit more of attention here, in the finishing' and you walk away. Don't worry. The message is going to reach the target. It works much better than trying doing it the way we do back home. You can't change the way they are. (Brazilian supervisor)

Some may see it just as a manipulative stratagem. I prefer to emphasize the sensibility of finding ways to achieve certain goals without disrespecting the codes of social behavior of the other group.

BEYOND INTERCULTURAL INTEGRATION

Over time, the intercultural integration effort leads to the formation of a common spirit, which may be translated in terms of common goals, shared feelings about the future and identification to the success of the organization:

> We work together very well because the two parts have the same goals. We both
> want to make things better … In both sides people want to do a better job. The feel-
> ing about the future is the same. (Chinese manager)

The differences between the two groups are always there, but the construction of a common identity is fundamental to achieve the tangible results that
improve their survival and success possibilities. A Chinese general-director
commented when referring to 'a common vision' and to 'a spirit of cooperation':

> After the production started, [a Brazilian] vice-president gave a speech and … said
> that the success of the joint venture could be explained by three factors: the
> common vision in terms of market and strategy, the existence of a spirit of cooper-
> ation, and the complementary strength of the two companies. I think he was right.
> (Chinese general-director)

And he was proud to tell me so.

CONCLUSION AND RECOMMENDATIONS TO PRACTITIONERS

In this chapter, I have tried to examine how some Sino-Brazilian organizations
in China have found their way to intercultural integration. As I observed and
questioned managers and workers in these companies, they started telling me
that Chinese and Brazilian were not that different. They were perhaps trying
to convince me – and themselves, for that matter – that they were 'naturally
close'. But do not fool yourself: they are culturally very far apart and they
went through difficult adaptations to work together.[5]

They have creatively combined disparate pieces from different national
cultures, working cultures, national histories and geopolitical projects to
develop 'discourses of proximity'. They have recognized the differences and
have given the other side the benefit of the doubt as they granted them 'intercultural slacks'. They have made sacrifices, left their comfort zones and put
together many different 'micro-dynamics of integration' to reach each other.
They have worked hard to bridge an entire world of differences.

Finally, as they have allowed themselves to coexist very closely, they have
discovered ways of interacting positively, acting without violating the other
cultural sensibility and have ended by creating a tradition of respect, collaboration and common spirit.

Many indeed have adopted a posture that resembles what anthropologists
call 'cultural relativism'. They have tried to appreciate and understand the
others' cultural tradition for what it was, to reflect on their own reactions and
to not use their own cultural conventions to judge others' cultures. They have

made a huge effort to create a positive climate, to empathize with 'the other', and to not burn the fieldwork as they have tried to leave a better stereotype behind them.

I am not saying that they were all playing the anthropologist but some were very conscious of their discoveries as they were being acculturated into the new setting.

Nevertheless, the final point here should be what may be learned from this study.

The specific steps they have taken have helped their intercultural integration. But these are not necessarily applicable to other multicultural organizations, to other South-South combinations or even perhaps to other cases combining Chinese and Brazilians. The proposed generic argument however shows that discourse and practice can be complementary. Despite the unquestionable cultural differences, people can work on similarities to build integration while, very much at the same time, acknowledging differences but not letting these be crystallized as positions of power or arguments of cultural superiority (for example, 'we know better' or 'our food is better'). Moreover, showing respect and sensibility towards 'the other', the eventual emerging hierarchical dispositions (as in teacher or boss) can be positively integrated to the local context.

I believe therefore that the main contribution of this chapter is to show that a 'discourse of proximity' might emphasize an integration intention that might, and should, be pragmatically supported by a combination of social norms, polices and widespread practices at the micro level.

WHY GO TO CHINA?

To close this chapter, I go back to where it started.

In the fieldwork, I many times asked the Brazilians the same question the Swede once asked his Italian colleague: 'So, why did you decide to come to China?' and I got all kinds of answers related to career goals, financial rewards and personal reasons. But what I really found fascinating were the things they told they had unexpectedly learned after actually getting there. Many passionately told me of their discoveries about the Chinese and their reality. Even more surprisingly, they also made many discoveries about themselves and about what it means to be Brazilian.

In conclusion to this chapter, perhaps one valuable bit of advice to an executive searching for people to work in multicultural organizations is: look for those who are willing and motivated to make sacrifices in order to learn about the others and about themselves. And, if your candidates ask you: 'So, why should I decide to go to Sweden?', you may now have a good answer.

NOTES

1. I am grateful for the financial support from Greville Smith Research Fellowship (McGill University), from Professor Henry Mintzberg's John Cleghorn Chair and from the McGill Center for Strategy Studies in Organizations that made this study possible. A broader study of these cases is presented as Chapter III of the doctoral thesis 'Cultural encounters in a global world', available at http://escholarship.mcgill.ca.
2. Respecting the research agreement, I must conceal all information that potentially identifies people, organizations, products, processes or technologies. The data has been collected mainly as notes taken during observations and interviews. Tape-recorded interviews were not always allowed or desired: top management had concerns about organizational politics and protection of 'industrial information' and employees tended to express a more 'official' or 'socially desired' version of their own opinions when exposed to tape-recording. Nevertheless, 19 open-ended interviews of about 50 minutes have been tape-recorded.
3. All quotes are from Brazilians and Chinese working for Sino-Brazilian joint ventures in China. Quotes originally in Portuguese have been translated into English.
4. *Cucaracha* is the Spanish word for cockroach. The interviewee refers to a pejorative term for a Latino-American migrant to more developed economies, particularly to the USA.
5. Space constraint made me give more emphasis to the Brazilians' adaptation, but the Chinese's effort to adapt to a new organizational context has also been condsiderable.

REFERENCES

Brannen, M.Y. (1996), 'Ethnographic international management research', in B.J. Punnett and O. Shenkar (eds), *Handbook for International Management Research*, 2nd edn, Cambridge, MA: Blackwell, pp. 115–43.

Byun, H. and S. Ybema (2005), 'Japanese business in the Dutch polder: the experience of cultural differences in asymmetric power relations', *Asia Pacific Business Review*, **11**(4), 535–52.

Hamada, T. (1991), *American Enterprise in Japan*, Albany, NY: State University of New York Press.

Pardi, T. (2005), 'Where did it go wrong? Hybridization and crisis of Toyota Motor Manufacturing UK, 1989–2001', *International Sociology*, **20**(1), 93–118.

Schein, E.H. (1996), 'Culture: the missing concept in organization studies', *Administrative Science Quarterly*, **41**(2), 229–40.

Schwartzman, H.B. (1993), *Ethnography in Organizations*, Newbury Park, CA: Sage.

11. Divorcing globalization from Orientalism: resembling economies and global value added

Iris Rittenhofer[1]

INTRODUCTION

The chapter offers an analysis of 'globalization' in corporate language use. As a concept, globalization does not denote a physical or material world. Rather, globalization denotes ways of thinking and perceiving (Scholte, 2000) the transforming relations between home and foreign markets. In an interdisciplinary approach, this chapter explores shared cultural patterns of perceptions and meaning production. These patterns reduce the complexity of globalizing markets to international business relations between distinct markets, and add to geographical distant markets the meaning of inferiority and economic weaknesses. This has implications for strategy development processes, in that these understandings of globalization limit the corporation's opportunities in a globalizing economy.

The chapter focuses on two cases. They are a visual and a textual representation revealing cultural patterns that inform corporate understandings of globalization. Representation is defined as 'the production of meaning of the concepts in our minds through language' (Hall, 1997, p. 17). Case 1 is a corporate actor's visualization of a global company. In Case 2, an expert gives investors advice on how to prepare for the opportunities of global markets. Both examples are chosen from qualitative Danish case material gathered by the author.[2] Both representations comprise an archive of information on shared patterns of perception and meaning production that widely inform corporate understandings of market relations and globalization.

CASE ANALYSIS

I apply Søderberg and Holden's (2002, p. 112) complex definition of culture to the analysis of globalization: I take an 'emergent, dynamic approach' to the conceptualization of globalization as 'made up of relations' and 'based on shared or partly shared patterns of meaning and interpretation'. Clusters of these patterns cross well-known boundaries as those of geographical areas to which they are neither limited to nor derive from. These patterns 'bear the burden of European thought and history' (Chakrabarty, 2000, p. 4). Accordingly, references to home or foreign markets are analysed as 'hyperreal': they present 'figures of imagination' (Chakrabarty, 2000, p. 27) rather than a material world. An example is the 'imagined communities' of nations (Anderson, 1983). Whenever I refer to either corporate or geographical entities in this chapter, I refer to hyperreal rather than physical unities.

Corporate language use is informed by an understanding of culture which is prescriptive, descriptive, functionalist and essentialist. The patterns found show that redundant meanings and interpretations of globalization burdened by European thought are closely linked to the imagination of the West as the sole driver of globalization and of its representatives (European nations, corporations) as natural capital and distinct value added in foreign markets and international trade. These patterns impact the practitioners' analysis and monitoring of the corporate environment.

I proceed to the case analysis, which is organized around the following patterns found in corporate thinking: internationalization and liberalization, Westernization, East and West, globality, territorialism, Orientalism and nation-ness. The respective paragraphs also point out how these patterns are intertwined and mutually reinforce each other.

CASE 1

Figure 11.1 is a visualized corporate narrative on globalization. The patterns behind this visualization contribute to the perpetual making of Europe in general, and Denmark and a Danish company in particular, the engine of international relations denoted as globalization.

Liberalization and Internationalization

An analysis of the slide reveals redundant understandings of globalization. Here, I focus on liberalization and internationalization.

Literally, this slide maps a 'globalized' corporation' which extends ten countries on several continents. These countries have something in common: they all are members of the World Trade Organization (WTO).[3] In 1995 set up to administer the GATT (Lynch 1997 [2003], p. 706), the aim of the international organizations WTO and GATT is to reduce restrictions on and to liberalize international trade.

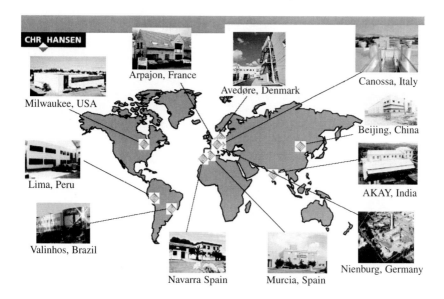

Figure 11.1   Slide: Chr. Hansen – the globalized corproration (author's translation)

Internationalization may be defined as 'increases of interaction and inter-dependence between people in different countries' (Scholte, 2000, p. 44). Liberalization means 'a world without regulatory barriers to transfers of resources between countries' (Scholte, 2000, p. 45). Both concepts rank among the redundant concepts of globalization: they do not open 'substantial new insights that have not been available through pre-existent terminology' (Scholte, 2000 pp. 44ff.). Here, liberalization and internationalization are understood as globalization.

Westernization

In this section I focus on a third redundant understanding of globalization, namely Westernization.

The arrangement of the connectors stage stakeholder relations. International relations are Westernized by the cluster of diamonds of the company logo. They create a centre of a world map and for the star-like arranged connectors. Connectors point in a one-way direction away from Europe and the West to the 'outside'. The arrangement of continents, logos and connectors represents the West, Europe, Denmark and 'its' company, as the only forces of globalization. Company, nation and the West are mutual representatives. Accordingly, the non-West is made the periphery of the West, imprinted by a Western company, but not a driving force of globalization in itself.

The slide in Figure 11.1 reveals an understanding of globalization as European-driven internationalization and liberalization, and a periphery affected in terms of Westernization. Since all three concepts are widely used, yet redundant understandings of globalization (Scholte, 2000), the slide may be said to be a redundant conceptualization of a company as global.

'East' and 'West'

A multifaceted Euro-centredness, reinforced by the concepts of East and West, is crucial for the understanding of an international company as global.

'Globalized' denotes the visible presence of Western corporate buildings at different locations in the East. 'East' and 'West' represent very complex concepts not primarily about place and geography (Hall and Gieben, 1992, pp. 276ff.). Like Europe, they have no simple or single meaning. Moreover, the concept of 'the modern' and the concept of 'the West' have identical meanings. The East is visualized as distant and made the other; it represents a periphery in terms of place and progress and thus acquires the meaning of being inferior to the West. This informs a cognitive limitation, namely that being a representative of the West, is a self-evident corporate competitive advantage in markets culturally seen as distant.

The Condition of Being Global

The slide visualizes a condition, rather than activities, and therefore not globalization, but rather globality.

Stakeholder relationships and foreign market entries are distanced from human activities. They appear to be the characteristic of a global condition beyond the reach and the control of humans. The title 'the globalized corporation' points towards the subjection of the company to globalization. Thus, globality is the adequate term to describe this condition. While globalization refers to the process of becoming more global, globality refers to the condition of being global (Scholte, 2000, p. 42). The term 'globalized' denotes that the company's globalizing process is concluded, and that the company's as-is state is global. This condition, however, is not innate, but constructed in the visualization. The making and the having of a global condition is mutually related. In order to be global, the condition of being global has to be achieved by giving new meanings to liberalization and Westernization of international stakeholder relations.

World System

The slide reveals a fourth redundant understanding of globalization, namely universalism.

The map centres stakeholder relations around a symbol for a Western capitalist enterprise. This reinforces the West as the sole driver of globalization, and excludes the possibilities of further drivers or diverse ways of organizing economic activity.[4] Corporate relations seem to be subjected to the 'overarching framework ... of the ... world-system' (Beck, 2000, p. 25): a capitalist world economy, redistributing resources from the periphery to the core. The globalized condition of the company is created on universalized capitalism. From this perspective, the term 'globalized' may be read as a symbolic legitimization of a capitalist enterprise expanding its economic sphere.

Territorialism and Linear Time

The slide reveals a corporate understanding of markets caught in the 'territorial trap' (Agnew and Corbridge, 1995), and which neither takes into account the borderless character of globalizing processes nor their effects on the home market.

Corporate relations are translated into spatial relations connecting separate units of territory. At the heart of the slide is territorialism: macro social space is perceived as wholly organized in terms of units such as towns, countries and continents (Scholte, 2000, p. 46). Territorial units represent the stakeholders of this company and of a representative of a nation and of the 'West'. In effect, the company appears to be a driver of homogenization that makes the world more Western and modern.

Criss-crossing globalizing processes are reduced to a rise in the number of corporate relations to physically distant and economically underdeveloped places.

The slide is burdened by the European idea that everything has to be seen as a condition, as a 'unity and in its historical development' (Chakrabarty, 2000, p. 6). Consequently, corporate stakeholders are perceived as distant, and corporate relations are translated into linear spatial and chronological developments. Spatiality, here the concept of home market is territorialized and historicized. The slide denotes an originally Danish company unfolding into a globalized one, and translates a historical development into expanded territorial relations. Globality denotes corporate relations spreading from a Western home market to Asian foreign markets perceived as distant in place and time.

In the visual and linguistic language of the slide emerges a narrative on corporate relations as 'something that became global over time, by originating in one place', namely, Europe, 'and then spreading outside it'. This '"first in

Europe, than elsewhere" structure' (Chakrabarty, 2000, pp. 7, 8) creates Europe and its corporation as 'first in time', the 'modern' and thus a driver of globalization. These patterns have long been well documented in politics and the humanities.

A key feature we find in corporate understandings is that globalization is added to a well-known model of international business: the Uppsala model.[5] In corporate perception, global means a company (gradually) moving from a culturally and territorially distinct and homogeneous home market in the West to an outside and equally distinct, yet distant foreign market. However, this linear and unidirectional understanding of internationalization does not capture multidirectional globalizing processes and the opportunities and challenges they create in transforming markets.

In Figure 11.1 globality is a matter of scale and thus a question of the number of foreign markets. A globalized company is expected to embrace a larger territory and thus denote a larger number of nations than an international company. Geographical distance is crucial in order to create the displayed notion of global-ness: the more of the distant markets, the more global is the company. Consequently, global is only happening 'outside' the home market. However, since globalizing processes are independent of territory and borders, their impact may be overlooked in the home market. Therefore, a global company's market may better be understood in terms of complex relations in a transworld space: the inhabited world perceived as one single unit.[6]

Orientalism

Due to cultural patterns that mutually reinforce each other, the slide visualizes an economy of resemblances rather than globalizing processes.

In order to produce the condition of being global, it is crucial to ask what nations are displayed in the slide. The perception of being global is in need of the presence of Eastern countries, due to meanings inherent to the concept of globalization itself. Globalization is the flipside of Orientalism. Both concepts are burdened by European thought. Globalization emerged as a critique of 'Orientalism' (Hastrup, 1999, pp. 213ff.). While Orientalism has the tendency to turn the unknown or distant other into a different and exotic other, globalization here means that the distant economically is transformed into the resembling other: globalization here rests on the assumption that this dissimilar other is merely a variation of the already known. As such, the basic approach to globalization was to critically point out that a 'them' actually are not unlike but do resemble an 'us', that 'the other' actually resembles 'the European' and Westerner. The liability of foreignness is overcome by creating economic resemblance of the East, that is, the production and sale of identical products by the same company in worldwide locations.

'Orientalism' is a well-known and widely recognized concept introduced by Edward W. Said in 1979 denoting the imperial gaze, which looks at disparity and dissimilarity as entirely different from and inferior to itself. 'The essence of Orientalism is the incradicable distinction between Western superiority and Oriental inferiority' (Said 1978 [2003], p. 42). A feature of 'oriental European relations was that Europe was always in a position of strength, not to say domination', and the essential relationship was seen in the West 'to be one between a strong and a weak partner' (Said 1978 [2003], p. 40). Orientalism is based on the perception of the Orient not being able to speak for itself and therefore to be understood from the outside.

In the slide, China and India constitute the exotic, but also the necessary 'other', since their presence stages the company and its relations as global. Corporate relations denoted as globalization transform the understanding of the foreign into the resembling market; business opportunities for the West emerge as a self-evident element of this global condition. United in the globalized company, the two East Asian countries resemble the European or Western company of origin in that they share stakeholder interests. Europe and its corporation are made a global centre, Asia a peripheral global player. Thus, resemblance is an issue of territorialized and orientalized relations which create dominance and subordination, core and periphery, and which dismiss multiplicity and connectivity. The perception of European superiority and a respective Eastern inferiority are linked to Europe as the symbolic modern represented by her companies in markets outside the West. As we shall see, it is precisely this relation which allows for the perception of nation-ness (Anderson, 1983) (here: Danish-ness) as a global value added.

The West First

Globalization is reduced to market homogenization in terms of product standardization, and international competition on price and quality.

'Orientalism is strongly linked to "the West first"' structure which allows for the perception of globalization as standardization. In the second case example on Danish and Chinese relations, globalization is defined as 'standardization' in terms of 'the fast duplicating of products in China', and cheap products in return, such as 'cheap t-shirts from China' (Hammeken, 2007, pp. 2, 13), or Danish cookies copied by the Chinese (Mathiasen, 2008). The 'Denmark first, then the outside' line of thought informs this understanding of globalization as the West exclusively setting standards in global trade and signifies Denmark as the stronger part in Danish/Chinese market relations. This pattern of thinking goes hand in hand with the time dimension: globalization develops from a point of originality, perceived as national territory and given the meaning of home market, and crosses distance to an exotic territory.

The patterns pointed out above add to the imagination of a home market as the territory of a Western nation and to the perception of nation-ness as a distinct value added.

CASE 2

[*Author's translation*] Even if we think that we produce the best products, they will still quickly be copied by China. The funny thing about globalization is that it often equals standardization ... So I think that we must create something original – something which is not easy to copy. Something cool, different, ugly, and authentic. (Hammmeken, 2007)

'She [a futurologist] talks about a homepage ... which offers home knitted baby-caps. There is a group of women in their grandma's age who earns good money by offering the parents of small children something which apparently is both, original and genuine.' Something which, signals time and vicinity. About the company, which produces mobile phones with an integrated compass, enabling Muslims always to find East. About the textile manufacturer, who makes 'praying-jeans' with a green thread, because this is a holy color in the Muslim world. All is done in the name of originality. And the buyer of an old car who sold it for additional charge because he discovered that it once was owned by the Pope.

Globalization is such an elastic word ... No matter how we interpret the word, it offers us a lot of opportunities – even for a small country such as Denmark with a small economy. We have grown accustomed to supplying value added to things. We have always done that, because we have no raw materials. That is why we constantly have to ask ourselves: do we produce original education? Do we work originally? Do we challenge ourselves, or do we simply do the same thing as everyone else? (Hammeken, 2007)

Nation-ness

This quote on globalization is based on the imagination of a national community and of nation-ness being a sustainable natural capital of global value. It reveals an understanding of globalization that reinforces nationalism. The idea of the ethnic origin and unchangeable character of Western nation-ness rests on eight myths (Smith, 1999, p. 192). These myths go hand in hand with Orientalism and stage nation as value added capable of competing successfully on a global scale. Together, both facilitate Denmark's position as an unchallenged global player dominant in relation to China.

The myth of origin in time ('always') roots Denmark in the mist of the timelessness of past and an eternal future. The myth of origins in space links the imagined nation to a state territory on a world map and organizes macro social space in terms of territorial units. Ancestry as a third myth is literally linked to the grandmothers and implicitly to the old craft of knitting.

Travelling products are the economic variant of the myth of migration. The myth of liberation lies in the confirmation of nation-ness continuing to be an asset in a global market. A fifth myth on greatness is a central characteristic of the imagined community and its corporate representatives as makers of global standards. This is reinforced by the pattern of 'us' and 'them' and linked to both Orientalism and to the Europe first construction. This leads to dependency: the original product comes first, the copy is only second; the compass comes first, prayers second. When globalization is denoted as standardization, globalization is in need of nation-ness, with the foreign market as its dependant. Thus, the condition of nation-ness makes a Western country appear in the light of an indispensable and irreplaceable engine of globalization.

Cheap Chinese copies represent the threat of national decline, the seventh myth of national origin. The threat may be turned down and the greatness of nation restored by producing originals which are less easy to copy – rebirth is the eighth myth of nation-ness. All eight elements are tied together by an evolutionary linear development and strengthened by examples for specific businesses representing the heroes which make nation-ness real. Since nation-ness is a product of nationalism (Anderson, 1983), nationalism may be said to be at the heart of this understanding of globality. Following the immanent logic of these cultural patterns, the appropriate way to meet the challenges of globalization is to become even more national.

These patterns transcend time; perceived as the eternal first, Denmark is associated with the seemingly natural origin of global products due to recurring successful practices of adding value. The root-thinking (Deleuze and Guattari, 1987) of success as deriving from and being contained in nation-ness makes it unique, distinct and thus unchallengeable. In effect, Denmark as a nation appears as an important player of globalization and a successful global front player. Authority, here an expert's voice, validates (Said 1978 [2003], pp. 21–32) these orientalized truths of Western and Danish supremacy.

Both case examples of corporate language use are caught in the territorial trap. The condition of nation-ness is intertwined with the condition of being global. These perceptions give no space for an understanding of globalization in terms of non-territorial, multidirectional, borderless and non-linear processes.

Orientalism and Nationalism Intertwined

The economic progress of the distant foreign market is made sense of as conditioned by the West and its representatives as the only driver of globalization.

Orientalism and nationalism are intertwined when China is made the imaginary second in terms of a lack and an absence of originality. Globality then is about the fulfilment of this incompleteness by Danish – read original – products.

Thus, China is put into 'an imaginary waiting room' (Chakrabarty, 2000, p. 8) of globalization – without Danish products, no Chinese global market activity. The lack of the original product, which China has to wait for in order to copy and sell, signifies the eternal pre-global condition of China commonly referred to as an emerging market. The original is by the time of its arrival in Asia an already well-known product, 'something which already has happened else-where, and which is to be reproduced mechanically or otherwise with a local content' (Chakrabarty, 2000, p. 8). In copying original Danish products, China resembles the West. China, however, also is the necessary distant in order to establish globality.

CORPORATE PERCEPTIONS VERSUS GLOBALIZING PROCESSES

The examples discussed here point to a line of corporate thinking that responds to cultural frameworks which predate a post-industrialized and a post-national world. The perceptions of globalization, as they are found in the case material, neither capture the complexity nor the transformations of contemporary complex and multidirectional transworld activities. They merely coexist.

Many scholars agree that the new phenomena we try to capture and under-stand as globalization actually are independent of national units. These phenomena 'cannot be situated at a fixed territorial location. They operate largely without regard of territorial distance' (Scholte, 2000, pp. 46ff.). Global relations are supranational relations, transborder exchanges without distance, transcending culture, economy and geography.

The elements which help identify Europe and its corporations as drivers of globalization and the West as a global value added are the same that reinforce Europe as the modern. These elements do not belong to European cultures; rather, they are burdened by European thought, but neither rooted in nor limited to geographical area and thus not territorial. These patterns Europeanize globalization, even though globalizing processes affect territo-ries, but do not derive from them.

The redundant concepts of globalization are neither specific for the corpo-rate community nor for Denmark. So states Scholte (2000, p. 46) that the four redundant concepts of globalization 'cover most academic, official, corporate and popular discussions of things "global"'. Scholte is a scholar with access to the 'g-words' (global, globalization and so on) in English language use alone. As this chapter demonstrates, the redundant concepts of globalization also are applied in Danish language use. Consequently, neither of the redundant concepts and cultural patterns discussed here can be territorialized and dismissed as distinctly Danish.

LEARNING POINTS FROM THE CASES

New phenomena cannot be understood in terms of shorthand descriptions which work both as reductive and prescriptive. Companies cannot act on complexity, transformations and lack of predictability in a globalizing world by monitoring the environment from the outset in seemingly self-evident and predefined frameworks, which belong to the world of first modernity, industrialization and powerful nation states. In order to update strategy development processes, practitioners need to understand cultural patterns and acknowledge the impact of sense-making processes on corporate thinking.

Redundant understandings of globalization, globality, territorialism, nation-ness and Orientalism are cultural patterns that mutually reinforce each other in the perception of globalization as a global economy of resemblances. As Tomlinson (2007, p. 151) observed, culture is consequential in that 'the processes of meaning construction inform, inspire and direct individual and collective actions which themselves are consequential'. This implies that if practitioners act on a territorialized and orientalized understanding of predefined units such as markets and stakeholders, they run the risk of making decisions on the grounds of imaginative competitive advantages. They risk neither to capture the complexity nor the connectivity of borderless transformations evoked by globalizing processes. If practitioners do not monitor complex economic relations, but rather see a global economy of resemblance, they impede the selection of new markets, as well as the analysis of transforming existing markets, home markets included.

Instead of focusing on conditions, practitioners need to refocus on market activities increasingly independent of boundaries. Globalizing processes are transnational and cannot adequately be understood by spatial and Euro-centred thinking that reduces multidirectional to bipolar corporate relations between distinct markets. Globalizing processes criss-cross all markets; accordingly, the dynamics of globalizing markets and companies cannot any longer be captured from the outset in the perception of markets as culturally distinct territories in terms of home and foreign markets. Practitioners run a risk, if they treat markets they perceive as distant or secondary to global developments less carefully than those they perceive as familiar and major global players.

RECOMMENDATIONS FOR PRACTITIONERS

What practitioners see is what they get. In order to build innovative corporate relations in a transworld space, globalizing activities need to be unburdened of

European thought, the concepts constitutive for redundant understandings of transworld activities.

Cultured perceptions are blind spots in strategy thinking. Since '[c]ultural signification and interpretation ... orient people ... towards particular actions' (Tomlinson, 2007, p. 151), the important point for cross-cultural management is to understand that monitoring processes are interpretations and perceptions of the corporation in its environment. Strategies are made by people who share or partly share 'conceptual maps' (Hall, 1997, p. 18) which cannot be separated from the perception and communication of facts. The monitoring and the analysis of the corporate environment therefore does not 'mirror' (Potter, 1996) facts, but makes sense of what is visible to us. Therefore, practitioners need to understand that monitoring and analytical processes are construction processes: they create the environment of the corporation.

A recommendable approach would be to integrate the tools and knowledge of complex cultural analysis into strategy development processes. Tools for cultural analysis have the potential to open up for diverse ways of value creation and the localization of stakeholder activities in a transworld space. This may be done by hiring cultural analytics to cooperate in multidisciplinary teams. In a globalizing world of growing complexity, this promises to impact on corporate understandings of global drivers and of global value added in a positive way. Moreover, in reflecting and altering their language use, corporate actors may positively contribute to the regulation of cultural knowledge on globalization. It would widen the scope of globalization strategies if practitioners would acknowledge that market relations are not to be reduced to territorial relations. Furthermore, practitioners need to develop a more contemporary understanding of market activities. Instead of looking for a global market, they ought to understand the transformations that connect market activities, both those perceived as familiar and those new to them. Finally, practitioners would need to develop relational and process-oriented understandings of transworld market activities that eventually may supersede the perception of markets in terms of geographical units and clear boundaries.

RECOMMENDATIONS FOR FUTURE RESEARCH

If strategy development processes rest on unrecognized assumptions which in turn affect corporate choice and decision making (Muller, 2004), there is a need to investigate the impact of these patterns on actual cross-cultural strategies developed by corporate managers not only in Europe. Collaborative research with an emergent dynamic approach to culture and a focus on culture's impact on the monitoring of transworld relations may therefore be of strategic importance for multicultural corporations. Furthermore, it might be of mutual interest for both research and companies to develop alternatives to spatialized perceptions of corporate relations in terms of cross-border reach. In addition, there is a need for future research to investigate into corporate language use as a site of economic competition and struggle for market shares. Moreover, research into comparative business issues has to be self-reflective and cautious not to reproduce the redundant patterns of thought themselves.

NOTES

1. This chapter is the reworked and much elaborated version of an oral paper given at the seminar 'Communication, media and management' at the international conference MatchPoints of Globalization, University of Aarhus, Denmark, 15–17 November 2007.
2. Sources are: DI (confederation of Danish Industries) http://www.di.dk publication from 21 September 2007, also to be accessed in a press release from 14 December 2007. 'Virksomhedernes Top 20 – når forskning skaber bundlinje' (Companies' top 20 – when research accomplishes bottom line). D/E/A Dansk Erhvervs Akademi, The Danish Business Academy, Copenhagen, November 2007. Nadia Mathiasen (2008), Kineserne kopier Danske småkager. *Nyhedsavisen*, Saturday 12 April 2008, p. 2. Lisbeth Ammitzbøll (2007), Dansker bag global klimaportal. *Magisterbladet* no. 18,16 November, pp.12–13. I want to offer special thanks for entrusting me his visualization of a globalized company in Figure 11.1 to Country Sales Manager D. Danielsen. It is of no importance to this contribution that the slide displays a Danish-based international company Chr. Hansen, which produces natural ingredient solutions for foods. Anette Hammeken (2007), Mug eller muligheder, *Investor. Medlemsblad for Danske Invest*, Thematic issue on globalization. March, pp. 12–13. Advert'Spar op i Sydinvest BRIK ...', *Weekendavisen* no. 12, 26 March 2010, Udland, p. 8.
3. Apart from China, who entered the organization in 2001, all countries on the map entered in 1995, when WTO was set to administer the General Agreement on Tariffs and Trade (GATT).
4. Chakrabarty (2000, p. 7) critically points out that nobody sees '"late capitalism" as a system whose driving engine may be in the third world'.
5. The Uppsala model describes a company's internationalization process. See Jan Johanson and Jan-Erik Vahlne (1990), 'The Mechanism of Internationalisation', *International Marketing Review*, 7(4), 11–24.
6. An understanding of globalizing processes requires a new approach to the market. A new understanding of market is developed in Rittenhofer and Nielsen (2009).

REFERENCES

Agnew, J. and S. Corbridge (1995), *Mastering Space. Hegemony, Territory and International Political Economy*, London and New York: Routledge.
Anderson, B. (1983), *Imagined Communities. Reflections on the Origins and Spread of Nationalism*, reprinted 1999, London: Verso.
Beck, U. (2000), *What is Globalization?*, Cambridge: Polity Press.
Chakrabarty, D. (2000), *Provincializing Europe. Postcolonial Thought and Historical Difference*, Princeton, NJ: Princeton University Press.
Deleuze, G. and F. Guattari (1987), *A Thousand Plateaus. Capitalism and Schizophrenia*, London and Minneapolis, MN: University of Minnesota Press.

Hall, S. (ed.) (1997), *Representation. Cultural Representations and Signifying Practices*, London: Sage.

Hall, S. and B. Gieben (1992), *Formations of Modernity*, Cambridge: Polity Press.

Hammeken, A. (2007), Mug eller muligheder, Investor. Medlemsblad for Danske Invest, Thematic issue of globalization, March, pp. 12–113.

Hastrup, K. (1999), V*iljen til Viden*, Copenhagen: Gyldendal.

Lynch, R. (1997), *Corporate Strategy,* reprinted 2003, London: Prentice Hall.

Mathiasen, N. (2008), Kineserne Kopier Danske Småkager, *Nyhedsavisen*, 12 April, p. 2.

Muller, R. (2004), 'Time, narrative and organizational culture: a corporate perspective', *TAMARA: Journal of Critical Postmodern Organization Science*, **3**(1), 1–13.

Potter, J. (1996), *Representing Reality. Discourse, Rhetoric and Social Construction*, London: Sage.

Rittenhofer, I. and M. Nielsen (2009), 'Marketscapes. Market between culture and globalization', *HERMES. Journal of Language and Communication Studies*, **43**, 59–95.

Said, E.W. (1978), *Orientalism,* reprinted 2003, London: Penguin Books.

Scholte, J. (2000), *Globalization – A Critical Introduction*, New York: Palgrave Macmillan.

Smith, A.(1999), *The Ethnic Origins of Nations,* Oxford: Blackwell.

Søderberg, A.-M. and N. Holden (2002), 'Rethinking cross-cultural management in a globalizing business world', *International Journal of Cross-Cultural Management*, **2**, 103–19.

Tomlinson, J. (2007), 'Globalization and cultural analysis', in D. Held and A. McGrew (eds), *Globalization Theory*, Cambridge: Polity Press, pp. 148–71.

12. Culture and negotiated meaning: implications for practitioners

Sonja A. Sackmann, Laurence Romani and Henriett Primecz

NEW WORK PLACE REALITIES

Over the past three decades, the business world has become increasingly inter-connected on a global scale (Chapter 11). Companies have internationalized or even globalized by establishing presence in different parts of the world – be it by developing representations (Chapter 7), sales offices and production sites in different countries (Chapters 3 and 8), by delivering services in different parts of the world (Chapter 2), by establishing strategic partnerships (Chapters 4 and 10) or by acquiring or merging with firms in different parts of the world (Chapter 5). A part of the workforce has become increasingly mobile moving around and working in different countries (Chapter 2). Hence, work places are composed of people from different regions and nations. The potential customers of many firms are also located in different parts of the world with customs and likings that are likely to differ from those of a company's home base.

Information is readily available worldwide through the word wide web and can be accessed in even the remotest area. This allows ideas and concepts such as management models to spread around the globe (Chapters 6 and 9) with still a strong dominance of Western conceptions (Chapter 11). Together, these factors have resulted in multicultural work situations that can be characterized by interactions between people of different regions, nations, organizations, professions, hierarchy, gender, ages and so on (Sackmann and Phillips, 2004).

Working effectively in such an increasingly multinational and multicultural business world on a global scale requires knowledge about these cultural differences as well as knowledge and skills about how to effectively deal with them not only in situations of business negotiations but also during everyday work processes. The ten cases in this book are good examples of the importance of being able to effectively work with such a cultural multiplicity and being attentive to the cultural specifics of the local context. Hence, it is no longer a luxury but a must to be able to navigate effectively such an ever more international, multinational and hence multicultural work environment. How can this be accomplished? Traditionally, people have used well-known cross-cultural dimensions, but these have their limitations as we discussed in Chapter 1 and briefly rehash below. Hence, we suggest in this volume a negotiated meanings perspective that brings context and richness to understanding intercultural interactions and thus goes far beyond cultural dimensions. In this final chapter, we briefly remind you of the principal limitations of the cultural dimension frameworks, and insist on the need to focus cross-cultural management on practices of interaction for effectively dealing with today's multicultural situations. We shall do so by first discussing some of the practical implications of the cases before we suggest nine strategies on how to better deal with or manage cultural dynamics within today's new work places and their cultural realities. We conclude with some caveats for working with and managing in a multiple culture context.

LIMITATIONS OF DIMENSIONAL FRAMEWORKS FOR UNDERSTANDING CULTURE SPECIFICS

A number of well-known so-called cross-cultural frameworks exist that focus on culture at the national level. They are used to characterize national cultures, compare them with each other and differentiate them from one another. Examples are the five dimensions by Kluckhohn and Strodtbeck (1961), the four and five bi-polar dimensions developed by Hofstede (1980, 2001), Schwartz' value system (1992), the dimensions developed and used in the Global Leadership and Organizational Behavior Effectiveness (GLOBE) project (for example, House et al., 1999, 2004) or the seven dimensions proposed and applied by Trompenaars (1994; Trompenaars and Hampden-Turner, 1998). While these dimensions give first indications of potential similarities and differences between nations, they have their limitations. First, they represent the statistical mean of the sample that was used for the development of the respective framework. As such, they refer to the majority in a normal distribution that may be associated with a stereotypical view. Stereotypes are helpful in that a few prominent characteristics are used for a first reading of a person or societal group at a, however, rather superficial level. They give a first impression that may not necessarily fit and that will definitely not capture the richness of a culture. In addition, these statistical averages may not apply to different regions or different societal groups of a given nation. They certainly will not apply to every person from a given nation.

As we have argued in more depth in Chapter 1, interacting and working effectively with people who have different cultural backgrounds requires a different approach in order to understand similarities and differences involved in the specific situation. The so-called cultural interaction and multiple cultures perspectives (for example, Boyacigiller et al., 2009) based on an interpretative paradigm (for example, Geertz, 1973) offer such an in-depth approach since they try to uncover phenomena and meaning systems from the standpoint of the people involved in specific interactions (Heider, 1959; Kelly, 1955).

As mentioned in the introductory chapter as well as Chapter 1, most contributions in this edited volume are based on such an interpretative perspective. The cases uncover, describe and analyse the underlying meanings that impact intercultural interactions of people involved in that particular work situation moving away from the level of national stereotypes. Even though the contributions originated from the work of researchers, the cases offer valuable insights for practitioners as pointed out at the end of each case. They also demonstrate that the interpretive intercultural interaction perspective is a powerful lens for practitioners in gaining a better understanding of multicultural interactions in work settings. Such an understanding is necessary for deciding on the most effective ways of working and dealing with cultural multiplicity at work.

In the following sections, we shall discuss some of the practical implications of the cases before we discuss nine strategies on how to better deal with or manage cultural dynamics within the context of work organizations.

NEGOTIATED MEANINGS PERSPECTIVE IN PRACTICE

When people of different nations act and interact with each other in the context of international, multinational or global organizations, at least two issues may become critical as illustrated in the cases included in this book. The first one is that what we think is obvious, visible and explicitly stated may not be that relevant or important to the people involved and for their actions. Second, organizational members act and interact with each other day in and day out, thus creating cultural dynamics with evolving meanings that do not necessarily fit well-known, static dimensions or textbook recommendations. We shall discuss these two issues in some more detail before we address their handling.

The Visible and Obvious Differences May Not be Important

International, multinational and globally acting firms create their products and services, mission and values statements, corporate and leadership guidelines, codes of conduct and practices and so on. One of the intentions underlying these statements and guidelines is to align their employees' actions with the company's overarching goals and intentions. Even though these codes of conduct and guidelines are well intended and usually 'communicated' or rather transmitted throughout the company, this rarely leads to a common understanding or even aligned actions. Since their content tends to be rather broad, it leaves room for local interpretations that may differ from the intended meanings – even if well intended. To give an example, in a multinational company, the leadership guidelines and associated selection procedures were transmitted to the different locations of the company. When these and related practices were discussed during a global management meeting, a leader located in Brazil was rather surprised when he learned about the intended meanings and practices reported by his colleague who worked in the firm's headquarter located in Germany. In Brazil, the same English words such as 'challenges people' were interpreted very differently leading to different practices both in regard to leadership behaviour and leader selection. Hence, the denotative meanings of the words in the code of conduct were not relevant but their connotative meanings were and those varied between locations. A similar case is reported in Chapter 5 by Christoph Barmeyer and Eric Davoine. Some of the German and French subsidiaries of the US-based firm overtly opposed the code of conduct that was developed in the firm's headquarters in the US. Even though subsidiaries were confronted with the same written (obvious) code, the specifics of their opposition can only be understood with detailed knowledge of the German and French environment, the sites' history and their relationship to the headquarters. Such knowledge would have helped taking actions in time to avoid the reported resistance to the normative content and legal association by the French and to the process of its development that did not consider German labour law. Chapter 6 by Hèla Yousfi reports a similar example that requires questioning the visible and obvious. A very successful Tunisian multinational appears to be successful due to its application of North American management techniques that are in contrast with traditional Tunisian management. Yet, when the author investigates how these techniques are applied in daily work in Tunisia, she discovers that the very success of these techniques was based on the fact that they were reinterpreted using traditional Tunisian views of organizations and organizing.

In addition, visible and observable behaviour is also interpreted from different cultural lenses in the context of international and multinational firms. This may lead to irritations due to different meanings associated with the same behaviour or due to normative expectations regarding how to behave properly. This is described, for example, in Chapter 4 by Sylvie Chevrier. Given their different conceptions of what is considered appropriate behaviour of an employee and of a superior, unintended misunderstandings emerged between French and Vietnamese colleagues in a non-governmental organization (NGO) operating in Vietnam. Likewise, Chapter 7 by Lisbeth Clausen reports that even though 'questioning the ordinary' is highly valued at the company's headquarter culture in Denmark, employees in the Japanese subsidiary had difficulties with this phrase since it was against a Japanese socio-cultural norm of fitting in, being part of and belonging to a group.

These selective examples show that even well-intended actions may lead to unintended misunderstandings because of the different interpretations made by people who were socialized into one or several different cultural contexts. Thus unintended misunderstandings are likely to happen because of people's different cultural imprint. Unfortunately, related problems tend to increase given the dynamics involved in the work place. The cases reported in this book give excellent examples of how unintended misunderstandings emerge over time and may lead to unforeseen realities and problems – in addition to their actual work.

Working and Managing in a Multinational Organization: Cultural Dynamics in Action

As we discussed in Chapter 1, individuals are creative human beings who construct their social reality. Their unique personal experiences such as the socialization processes within the context of a specific nation, region, profession and organization provide them with a unique cognitive scheme that helps them perceive, read and understand whatever happens around them. Hence, the chances are rather slim that people from a different cultural background working together have and use the same meaning systems to make sense of what they experience in their daily interactions. Hence, when the US-based company AMIE transferred their ethical code to their locations in France and Germany, different reactions followed – even in the same country (Chapter 5). Given the different history of the Frankfurt and Hamburg location with their US owner, the people in Frankfurt were amenable to accepting the code once it was adapted to fit the German legal context while people at the Hamburg location remained very critical given the dominant role that AMIE had played during the merger. The unique cognitive scheme that they had developed in this site kept influencing the employee's views on the code.

People may be creative in dealing with the cultural differences at hand in ways that evolve and that are not predictable. Under certain conditions such as having to interact, they may enter a negotiation process about their joint work reality and create a modus operandi or joint culture that acknowledges their critical needs while allowing room for cultural specifics. Guilherme Azevedo (Chapter 10) gives examples of practices of how the members of the Sino-Brazilian organization developed a joint working culture despite coming from apparently cultural antipodes. As early research in social psychology suggests, having to interact with each other or, as Guilherme Azevedo suggests, practices of micro-integration may foster common understanding and discover common grounds and a sense of proximity.

These new understandings and cultural practices emerge over time as a result of interactions and they may reveal growing acceptance of the otherness also described in the case by Lisbeth Clausen. Even though the Japanese partners had difficulties accepting the expected behavior of 'questioning the ordinary' valued by the Danish headquarters, over time they developed an understanding of the underlying concept. The regional manager even decided to develop and use a second organization chart in order to fit the needs of both the Japanese and the Danes. While the Danes preferred the matrix chart that showed responsibilities, the Japanese felt more comfortable with the chart that showed the hierarchical order indicating the personal standing within the hierarchy.

In sum, the interaction of people from different cultural backgrounds builds on the cognitive schemes they have developed, as well as the ones they create. The following section centres on the development of successful intercultural interactions. We discuss nine strategies that are essential in working effectively in a multiple culture context – be it in the role of an employee or of a manager.

DEALING WITH AND MANAGING CULTURAL MULTIPLICITY AND RELATED DYNAMICS – NINE STRATEGIES TO BE EFFECTIVE

The cases described in this book contain several recommendations for dealing effectively with cultural differences, cultural multiplicity and cultural dynamics. They can be summarized with nine strategies as shown in Figure 12.1.

When working in a setting with multiple cultures, cultural differences should be expected rather than being seen as a surprise. Working with people effectively who have different cultural backgrounds requires knowing the cultural meaning systems or frames that are relevant in a given setting. This entails identifying the interpretation mechanisms and gaining an understanding from the point of view of the natives or locals. Since differences will exist, people who can act as interpreter and mediator of meaning between the various cultures involved are essential. Finding and identifying common grounds between the cultures involved is a start to developing mutual understandings and negotiated meanings. Despite common grounds, people need to not only show respect for the otherness but also appreciate other perspectives and learn from them. A common spirit or goal known by the people involved – who also identify with it – will help in overcoming differences and enable effective cooperation. Nevertheless, politics at the individual, group and organizational level as well as differing institutions may impact cross-cultural cooperation and turn even prior effective ones into problematic ones. This implies that a manager needs to also be aware of the larger context in which interactions take place. We shall now discuss these nine strategies in more detail.

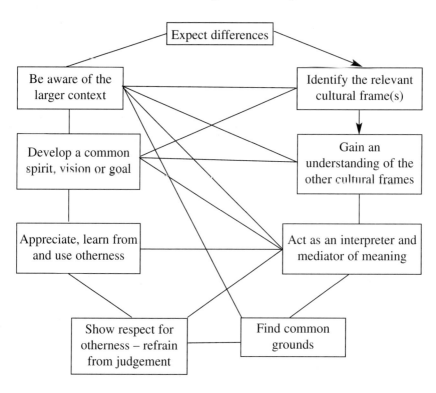

Figure 12.1   Managing cultural multiplicity and related dynamics

Expect Differences

By definition, multinational firms are located in various nations that bring differences into the company. Despite worldwide branding and attempts to align organizational members' behaviour, differences will exist between locations due to their differing geographical and societal context. When people of different backgrounds work together, they bring with them their unique culturally influenced experience. The more diverse the group, the more people have moved around having worked in different companies, regions and nations, the more cultural variety will exist. Nevertheless, we are often surprised when people think and act differently from ourselves. But in fact, why should the people in Germany and France behave like Americans given their different history? Why should Vietnamese and French have the same expectations of a 'good' leader and appropriate employee behaviour? Why should the Japanese behave like the Danes or the Brazilians like the Chinese? Why should engineers think like managers? Why should Bulgarians have the same view on entrepreneurship as Western Europeans? Why should a Western perspective fit around the globe? Hence, a better strategy than expecting sameness is to expect differences and look out for them.

Identifying the Relevant Cultural Frames

Expecting cultural differences is, however, not sufficient in working effectively in a multicultural work setting. The question is: what kinds of cultural frames or meaning systems do exist and which ones are relevant in a given situation? As discussed above, people tend to automatically expect cultural differences based on nationality and visible differences. These may, however, be rather misleading as illustrated in Chapter 8 and our own research. Sonja Sackmann was asked by a multinational firm to help with an anticipated joint venture between parts of the German and the French organization. When looking into the history of the firm, the prior difficulties were, however, rather based on different organizational cultures due to a prior merger between two companies as well as regional differences within the same country. Nevertheless, organizational members referred to difficulties with the other nation because intercultural problems between the French and the Germans were acceptable and readily available labels. People involved were not able to recognize these subcultural differences within their firm because of a lack of respective cognitive categories, nor had they developed labels for addressing them verbally.

In the case presented by Jasmine Mahadevan (Chapter 8), German engineers felt closer to their Indian engineering colleagues than to their German managers or human resources (HR) colleagues. Their socialization into the engineering profession did not only furnish them with English as the common language for interactions at work but also with a way of thinking and approaching problems that differed from other professions such as the HR people within the same company. The case by Lisbeth Clausen (Chapter 7) also shows that different kinds of subcultures may be of relevance to people at different times. In AMIE, the Germans did not only resist in a different way than the French did to the US-based ethical code, they reacted rather differently in the two German locations based on their different history with the US-based owners.

Rather than acting on obvious and therefore socially acceptable stereotypes that may, however, be misleading, practitioners need to find out which ones are the relevant cultural identifications and subgroups in a given setting and situation. This requires getting involved and being knowledgeable about the setting without preconceived ideas – hence, the need to act like an ethnographer. An ethnographer gets immersed in a given setting trying to find out relevant aspects in that setting while bracketing own assumptions and delaying judgment. This requires both curiosity and sensitivity in order to be able to see the multifaceted cultural reality. As the regional manager in Japan (Chapter 7) stated, 'sensitivity is one of the major elements in intercultural competence'. At times, however, the dominant culture frame such as our Western world view (Chapter 11) may be so prevalent that it is rather difficult to bracket or escape it.

Gaining an Understanding of the Others' Cultural Perspective

In addition to expecting differences and identifying the relevant ones, it is also important to be able to read and understand the different cultural perspectives. It requires being able to make sense of the viewpoint of the others from their 'native' perspective, thus moving from a position of ethnocentrism towards a position of ethnorelativism. The cases reported by Christoph Barmeyer and Eric Davoine (Chapter 5), Snejina Michailova and Graham Hollinshead (Chapter 9), Sylvie Chevrier (Chapter 4) and the second case of Sampo Tukiainen (Chapter 3) and even the discussion by Iris Rittenhofer (Chapter 11) give examples of ethnocentrism in action. People involved in interactions did not understand the others' cultural frames and related behaviours. Assuming that an ethical code has the same meaning in different countries (Chapter 5) or that managerial training programmes can be transferred to different countries without acknowledging the respective cultural contexts (Chapter 9) are rather ethnocentric approaches. Such an ethnocentric approach results in confusion in all actors involved as shown in the case by Sylvie Chevrier (Chapter 4). The Vietnamese employees did not understand why the French managers acted as they did nor did the French managers understand the behaviour of the Vietnamese employees. If people involved in such intercultural interactions are not willing to or are not capable of moving beyond their own cultural understanding, trying to see and make sense of the world from the perspective of the others, these misunderstandings will not be resolved. The cases by Jasmine Mahadevan (Chapter 8) and Sampo Tukiainen (Chapter 3) illustrate situations of both ethnocentrism and of mutual understandings including the respective effects of both positions. In the first project between the Finns and Poles, people involved could overcome their cultural differences and achieve their respective and the firm's objectives. In the second case, their local inter- ests differed and were more important to people than the firm's overall objec- tive, thus preventing them from building on the common understandings they had developed and practiced in the first project (Chapter 3). When German HR professionals interacted with the Indian engineers, work-related problems would pertain and be attributed to the national differences (Chapter 8). When the engineers interacted, however, with the managers who also had an engi- neering background, they could resolve disputes over deadlines and so on because they were able to understand each other's points of views since the managers were once engineers too.

How one can move from ethnocentrism to ethnorelativism and develop into an interculturalist who is able to understand people with other cultural backgrounds is illustrated in the cases by Guilherme Azevedo (Chapter 10), Lisbeth Clausen (Chapter 7) and the first project reported by Sampo Tukiainen (Chapter 3). As Lisbeth Clausen (Chapter 7) reports in the case of the Danish acquisition of the Japanese partner, the 'cultural transformation requires a deep understanding of both cultures involved'. Such an understanding can be gained by finding some common ground and building on similarities as suggested by Phillips and Sackmann (2002). As Guilherme Azevedo describes, the absence of a negative stereotype is already a good start that can be followed by constructing a sense of proximity (Chapter 10). This is a mutual effort in which similarities in behaviour and values are uncovered. Time and opportunities for interactions are important in helping develop such a mutual understanding. These may not only occur during formal work. Instead, informal settings such as spending time together during meals, joint sports activities and celebrations are very important for developing bonds and thus gaining a better understanding of each other.

Acting as an Interpreter and Mediator of Meanings

When people from different cultural backgrounds interact at work, their different perspectives may lead to unintended misunderstandings, problems, conflicts and inefficiencies as shown in several cases of this edited volume. Next to expecting differences, recognizing them and understanding their underlying meanings from the perspective of the so-called natives or insiders, it is important to also be able to bridge those differences so that people can work effectively with each other. As the office manager in the case by Lisbeth Clausen (Chapter 7) states: 'One way to think about my role is that of an interpreter', and an important responsibility of the office manager turned out to be that of a mediator between the firm's headquarters in Denmark and the Japanese office.

Being able to serve as an interpreter between different cultures requires, however, an understanding of the native perspective of the (sub)cultures involved. His growing understanding of the needs of the Danish and Japanese employees made the manager decide to develop and maintain two organizational charts depicting responsibilities for the Danes in the matrix and showing recognition and the place of belonging within the hierarchy for the Japanese. Another example is given in Chapter 8: only because the managers had also been engineers could they understand the perspective of the engineers in contrast to the HR professionals who did not have the engineering background.

If the manager, team leader or another person of an organization cannot take the role of the interpreter or mediator because they are a member of the same interaction system and too close to the issues at hand, it may be worthwhile involving an external facilitator. An external facilitator can act in that role and help recognize similarities and differences, thus fostering mutual understanding. This was the case during the first collaboration between the Finnish and Polish teams presented in Chapter 3. Sonja Sackmann was once asked to help the newly formed top management team of a Swiss-US joint venture. They felt that their differences were so great and the goals for the joint venture so different that they needed help with developing their top executive team. Before starting with the team development, she interviewed all top executives individually to find out about their respective views of the situation and goals for their joint venture. Surprisingly, the individual interviews revealed that all top executives had basically the same goals for the joint venture but the people involved were not able to recognize that. Instead, they interpreted all contributions and actions from people of the other national and organizational culture as being adverse. When she presented her findings to the top management and gave the respective feedback to them, they were rather surprised. The team development was no longer necessary.

Finding Common Grounds

When people with different cultural backgrounds meet, a natural behavior is to stick with people from the same group as described in the introductory section by Guilherme Azevedo (Chapter 10) and assume differences based on known and accepted stereotypical views. If people need to work together such as in the Sino-Brazilian firm, in the Danish company operating in Japan or within the context of the NGO operating in Vietnam, it will help if some common grounds between the cultures involved can be identified despite all the noticeable differences. Such a common ground helps in tackling difficulties in a more constructive way and developing appreciation for each other (Phillips and Sackmann, 2002). Even though the Danish company was physically far away from the Japanese subsidiary, simplicity turned out to be the common denominator of both organizations (Chapter 7). Having this important common ground helped people from both cultures work with their differences. Coming both from countries that are similar in their development was a helpful common denominator in the Sino-Brazilian company. They were rather creative in identifying additional commonalities such as being generous to those that visit them, being friendly, talkative and noisy, having a sense of humor, loving football/soccer but also working hard and seriously (Chapter 10).

Show Respect for Otherness and Refrain from Judgment

Despite all the common ground that can be identified, people with different cultural backgrounds will continue to be different. The question then becomes: how are these differences treated? Are they detested, negated or tolerated? Frequently, people act on the implicit assumption that their own perspective is the best – because it is familiar to them – and the other perspective, the unfamiliar, is evaluated as being inferior. Even if unintended, such an attitude shows in daily interactions. Mutual respect for the otherness is therefore one of the most critical aspects in intercultural encounters. It also needs to be based on a level of partnership without making a judgement about who is superior or inferior.

The cases by Guilherme Azevedo (Chapter 10), Lisbeth Clausen (Chapter 7) and Sara Louise Muhr and Jeanette Lemmergaard (Chapter 2) describe such a mutual respect between the actors involved and the resulting effective ways of collaboration. In the case of the Sino-Brazilian organization, both the Brazilian and the Chinese managers acknowledge that they needed to adapt and that it was hard for people from both cultures. They state: 'here we respect and accept the differences on both sides' (p. 118). How difficult it may be at times is well captured in the story about adapting to Chinese food and how the Brazilian manager managed to develop a strategy so that he could better cope with the situation, not showing his disrespect towards the Chinese colleagues.

In the case of the AV Company, the Japanese accepted the basic Danish value of questioning the ordinary without judging it as bad even though they considered it against their culture (Chapter 7). Respect towards the other is also expressed by the international consultant: 'I talk to the eyes I see, and whether they are placed in a man or a woman or a black or a white doesn't really mean anything to me … I very quickly got the nickname "color" blind' (p. 22).

Furthermore, Chapter 11 by Iris Rittenhofer suggests that we should also question our prominent and still dominant Western world view when interacting and conducting business with people from other parts of the world or acting in other parts of the world.

Appreciate the Otherness – and Learn from Each Other

Developing mutual respect towards the other cultural perspectives is important but not sufficient for most effective cooperation at work. It implies tolerance towards each other allowing people involved to co-exist. Effective intercultural interaction and cooperation moves a step further towards appreciating the otherness and even learning from each other. The case by Hèla Yousfi (Chapter 6) describes, for example, how the employees of the Tunisian company reinterpreted the US-based management tools and applied them in a way that benefited their organization. The case of Western management training in Eastern Europe (Chapter 9) also shows growing acceptance of the existence of local specifics and how this knowledge was used for developing more effective management training programmes. The case in Chapter 4 shows how the partners draw on each other's complementarities to become more effective in the project. Likewise, Guilherme Azevedo reveals how Brazilian managers appreciate and use Chinese communication styles and show respect towards the individual worker when they want to correct a production mistake (Chapter 10).

Develop a Common Spirit, Vision or Goal

Some of the cases also illustrate that having a common vision, spirit or goal for the organization composed of multiple cultures helps overcome cultural differences and difficulties that may emerge despite all the respect and appreciation for each other. This common goal needs to be, however, accepted by the people involved. In the first project reported by Sampo Tukiainen, the common goal of the organization was known and accepted by both the Poles and the Finns, but not in the second one due to different local interests. Despite their successful cooperation in the first project, the Finns wanted to make sure that the new technology would work while the Poles also wanted to maintain as many jobs as possible in the Polish location.

In the Sino-Brazilian joint venture (Chapter 10), Chinese and Brazilians worked together well because they had the same goals. According to the Chinese manager, they both wanted to make things better. The Chinese general director and the Brazilian vice-president also agreed in that a successful joint venture is based on a common vision in terms of market and strategy, the existence of a spirit of cooperation, and the complementary strength of the two companies.

Be Aware of the Encompassing Context

In addition to expecting differences, identifying the relevant cultural frames and their related differences, gaining an understanding of the other culture frames and perspectives, acting as an interpreter and mediator of meanings, finding common grounds, showing respect for otherness, appreciating and learning from each other and developing a common spirit or goal, a manager also needs to be aware of the larger enveloping context in which a given intercultural interaction takes place. This encompassing context may consist of differing interests due to politics at the individual, group and organizational level as well as differing institutions. It may present a power unbalance between the partners or be influenced by previous interactions between them.

Although people at the micro-level of interaction are well intended in their daily interactions with people coming from different cultural backgrounds, political interests may get in their way. The cases by Jasmine Mahadevan and Sampo Tukiainen show that, for example, fear about losing one's job may prevent well-intended people from sharing their knowledge with employees from the other culture and/or location. Why should the German engineer continue transferring his knowledge to the Indian location if the Indian colleague – who took over his job – is performing better? Why should the Polish manager accept the Finns taking charge of the project if his primary goal is to keep as many jobs as possible in his location in times of high levels of unemployment?

Next to political interests at the organizational level, institutions also influence cultural interactions. Hence, their interests, role and potential influence need to be considered by multinational firms, otherwise unexpected problems may arise. The case by Christoph Barmeyer and Eric Davoine illustrates how normative management instruments such as a code of conduct need to be adjusted to the local context. Intended for introducing (US) ethical standards and streamlining behavior across the different locations of a multinational company, nationally different laws and regulations need to be taken into account. In addition to different interpretations of what is considered ethical, the legal implications need to be known. Relevant institutions may differ across countries. The German worker's council is not known in the USA but critical in German companies with legal implications such as workers' participation in decision making and their representation on the board.

WORKING IN A MULTIPLE-CULTURE CONTEXT – SOME CAVEATS

The above nine strategies are helpful in developing effective intercultural work relationships. Nevertheless, there are a few caveats that need to be observed. First of all, when encountering people with different cultural backgrounds, it is important not to act on established, visible or well-known stereotypes since they may be misleading. People of dark colour may have been raised and socialized in a predominantly white society. Women may have been trained in a stereotypically male profession and a passport may not be that relevant to the cultural identity of the passport holder. Thus, one needs to be open towards the interaction partner and find out those relevant cultural identifications that are not necessarily visible or that are 'below the skin'.

As we mentioned above, it is also important to be open to the unfolding dynamics in intercultural interactions. One situation may differ from the next, interests may be different and power constellations may change. A once successful cooperation may change into a difficult one as illustrated in the case by Sampo Tukiainen.

In addition, research has shown that working successfully in an intercultural and multicultural setting requires resilience and knowledge about one's own cultural identity. As several cases illustrate in this book, working with people from other cultures may also lead to finding out more about oneself. Despite all cultural sensitivity, it is important to accept that one is different from the others and that one does not need to adapt to everyone's differing expectations. Building on some common ground, respecting and appreciating otherness is also important in regard to one's own cultural identity and psychological sanity.

In the case of crossing cultural boundaries frequently, actively searching out for culturally generic spaces may be an effective coping strategy as described by Sara Louise Muhr and Jeanette Lemmergaard. These spaces such as airports and airport lounges, international hotel chains or conference centres do not require cultural understanding – they are known to the frequent traveler and thus feel familiar no matter where they are located around the globe. In fact, for many years it was the strategy of US-based fast-food and hotel chains to build their premises on the same type of street intersection throughout the US, use the same architecture, the same interiors and food choices, have service people dress the same so that the frequent traveller such as sales agents would feel right at home. Amidst augmenting inter- and multicultural interactions, it is increasingly important to find physical and emotional spaces and time for maintaining one's own cultural identity and psychological sanity.

CONCLUSION

Today's work places are composed of a mix of cultures, either in terms of the cultural background of the interacting people or the practices they have developed by working together in a strategic alliance such as a joint venture. Working successfully in our increasingly multinational and multicultural business world requires that people are able to effectively deal with intercultural interactions. The ten cases in this book show the relevance of being agile in intercultural interactions, illustrating also the various forms of culture that can be relevant. We present in this volume a negotiated meanings perspective that goes beyond the cultural dimension frameworks to explain what is going on in practice, and therefore how to effectively manage interactions. The nine strategies introduced in this chapter encapsulate and summarize many of the insights and implications from the cases, and provide a guide for action in intercultural interactions, for cross-cultural management in practice.

REFERENCES

Boyacigiller, N.A., M.J. Kleinberg, M.E. Phillips and S.A. Sackmann (2009), 'Conceptualizing culture. Elucidating the streams of research in international cross-cultural management', in T.G. Andrews and R. Mead (eds), *Handbook of Cross-Cultural Management* (reprinted from the *Handbook of International Cross-Cultural Management*, 2006), Routledge, pp. 371–80.

Cohen, L. and A. El-Sawad (2007), 'Lived experiences of offshoring: an examination of UK and Indian financial service employees' accounts of themselves and one another', *Human Relations*, **60**(8), 1235–62.

Geertz, C.J. ([1973] 1993), *The Interpretation of Cultures*, New York: Basic Books, reprinted London: Fontana Press.

Heider, F. (1959), 'On perception, event structure, and psychological environment', *Psychological Issues*, **1**(4), 1–123.

Hofstede, G. (1980), *Culture's Consequences: International Differences in Work-related Values*, Beverly Hills, CA: Sage.

Hofstede, G. (2001), *Culture's Consequences: Comparing Values, Behaviors, Institutions and Organizations Across Nations*, Thousand Oaks, CA: Sage.

House, R.J., A. Delbecy and T.W. Taris (1999), *Value Based Leadership: An Integrated Theory and an Empirical Test*, Sidney: University of New South Wales Press.

House, R.J., Hanges, J. Paul, M. Javidan, P.W. Dorfman and V. Gupta (eds) (2004), *Culture, Leadership and Organizations: The GLOBE Study of 62 Countries*, Thousand Oaks, CA: Sage.

Kelly, G.A. (1955), *The Psychology of Personal Construct Theory, Vol. 1: A Theory of Personality*, New York: Norton.

Kluckhohn, F.R. and F.L. Strodtbeck (1961), *Variations in Value Orientations*, Evanston, IL: Row, Peterson.

Phillips, M.E., S.A. Saekman and R.A. Goodman (1992), 'Exploring the complex cultural milieu of project teams', *PM Network – Professional Magazine of the Project Management Institute*, **4**(8), 20–26.

Phillips, M.E. and S.A. Sackmann (2002) 'Managing in an era of multiple cultures', *The Graziadio Business Report*, accessed 18 November 2010 at http://gbr.pepperdine.edu/024/multi-cultural.html.

Sackmann, S.A. and M.E. Phillips, (2004), 'Contextual influences on culture research: shifting assumptions for new workplace realities', *IJCCM International Journal of Cross-Cultural Management*, **4**(3), 370–90.

Schwartz, S.H. (1992), 'Universals in the content and atructure of values: theory and empirical tests in 20 countries', in M.P. Zanna (ed.), *Advances in Experimental Social Psychology*, vol 25, New York: Academic Press, pp. 1–65.

Schwartz, S.H. (1994), 'Beyond individualism/collectivism: new cultural dimensions of values', in U. Kim, H. Triandis, Ç. Kâğitçibaşi et al. (eds), *'Individualism and Collectivism': Theory, Method and Applications*, London: Sage Publications, pp. 85–119.

Trompenaars, F. (1994), *Riding the Waves of Culture: Understanding Cultural Diversity in Business*, Chicago, IL: Irwin.

Trompenaars, F. and C. Hampden-Turner (1998), *Riding the Waves of Culture: Understanding Cultural Diversity in Business,* 2nd edn, Chicago, IL: Irwin.

Index